THE AIR FRYER COOKBOOK FOR BEGINNERS

250+ Easy, Delicious, Budget-Friendly & Healthy Recipes You Can Make Effortlessly Using Your Air Fryer

By

Fearne Prentice

A BOOK FROM THE

COOKING WITH FEARNE

SERIES

A BOOK FROM THE
COOKING WITH FEARNE
SERIES

The Air Fryer will change the way we cook and eat forever!

The Air Fryer emerged from frustrations with the unhealthy consequences that fried food has for our health. Fred van der Weij, a Dutch inventor, worked for 5 years on what is now known as the Air Fryer.

This book consists of 12 different sections, each complete with comprehensive recipes and a list of required ingredients. You'll never need another Air Fryer cookbook again!

Thank you for buying this book by Fearne Prentixe today, and don't forget to stay tuned for more recipes under the "Cooking with Fearne" series!

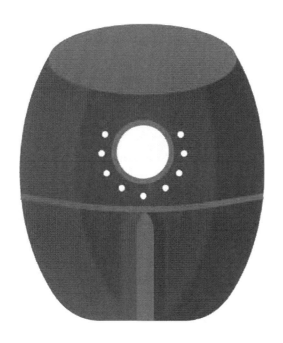

TABLE OF CONTENTS

13 | DESSERTS 141

ABOUT THE AUTHOR 152

1 | INTRODUCTION

We're crazy about the crispness that fried food can offer, and now there's a way to enjoy your favourite fried meal without heavy oxidised oil.

The Air Fryer emerged from frustrations with the unhealthy consequences that fried food has for our health. Fred van der Weij, a Dutch inventor, worked for 5 years on what is now known as the Air Fryer.

Today, there are many different manufacturers, and an Air Fryer is easily accessible for every household.

In this book you will find over 250 tasty recipes that are easy to prepare and don't require any previous cooking knowledge.

WHAT IS AN AIR FRYER?

An Air Fryer has a unique format that enables it to produce perfectly crispy dishes. As an air frying machine, it uses air to dry the outer part of a meal, while heating methods ensure perfect baking on the inside.

It will usually look like a mini oven, with one tray for cooking food. The temperature can be adjusted while your food is cooking, and you can always pause the frying to stir, turn or check on your dish.

HOW DO YOU OPERATE AN AIR FRYER SAFELY?

Once you have received your Air Fryer, make sure to remove all the packaging and read all the instructions.

Position it a little way out from your kitchen wall. This is very important as the hot air that is pushed out of the Air Fryer is directed through the back of the machine.

Now, time for testing! Run the machine for 2 minutes without food – this way you can check that your machine is heating properly and working smoothly. If the tray is hot after the test, then you're ready for your first recipe.

COOKING TIPS

The Air Fryer can "fry" many different dishes using nothing but a little oil. While some recipes will recommend no oil, we would recommend just a little in most cases, to prevent the dish sticking to the Air Fryer.

When selecting an oil, consider avocado, sesame, or sunflower oils, as they have a very high heating temperature. Test it out on your cooking tray before you add any food, and you'll prevent your tray from suffering scratches.

In this book, you will find many cooking recipes with suggested preparation times and instructions. Just remember, when you start to cook your own recipes, take care how much food you add to the cooking tray – it should never be overloaded.

The tray should only ever be filled halfway, so that air can circulate and ensure the food is crispy and crunchy.

HOW SHOULD YOU MAINTAIN YOUR AIR FRYER

Never use metallic kitchen utensils that may scratch or destroy your cooking tray – if necessary, just give it a shake to test food readiness.

You'll only need a soft sponge and dish soap to clean your tray – never use a scratchy material, such as steel wool. If food has stuck to the tray, soak it in hot water for 15 minutes.

To clean the surface of your Air Fryer, just use a water sprayer and soft cotton towel. This will ensure that you prolong the life of your Air Fryer.

SOME COMMON MISTAKES

An Air Fryer is super easy to work with and you should be perfectly safe using it at home. However, there are some common mistakes:

- Adding too much food – this can lead to soft and mushy baked recipes.

- Using spray oil – this can lead to cooking tray damage.

- Not checking your food – the Air Fryer allows you to open it throughout the cooking process, without dropping in temperature. If you don't check your food as it's cooking, you risk burning it.

- Not cleaning the cooking tray after every use – yes, the capacity of an Air Fryer is smaller than a regular oven pan and you will need to cook some recipes in batches. However, try to clean your cooking tray after every use.

FAQS

Can I Use Oil in my Air Fryer?

According to CDC (The Centers for Disease Control and Prevention) norms, overweight Excessive oil usage is not necessary with an Air Fryer. However, it is a good idea to spread a little oil on the basket.

Can I Mix Food in my AirFryer?

It depends on the type of basket you have in your Air Fryer. If you have two separate baskets, then it is okay to mix separate foods.

If you are cooking a recipe that combines ingredients, it is okay to add them to the basket together. The only time when you should not mix two different ingredients in an Air Fryer is if you don't want the flavours to be mixed.

What Kind of Foil Should I Use in my Air Fryer?

Using aluminium foil in your Air Fryer will help you to keep the basket cleaner for longer.

You can also use baking paper for pastries or baked goods. Other types of foil are not recommended for usage in the Air Fryer.

What Kind of Cooking Pans Can I Use in my Air Fryer?

There are many different types of cooking pans created specifically for the Air Fryer basket.

Here is a list of approved materials that you can use in the Air Fryer:

- Heat proof glass
- Silicone moulds
- Aluminium
- Stainless steel
- Cast ceramic

Does an Air Fryer require more electrical energy than my oven?

This answer mostly depends on the size of the Air Fryer. However, because of their fast cooking times, Air Fryers are generally more economical than a traditional oven.

Which Air Fryer should I purchase?

There are many different types of Air Fryers, and quality varies. The type of Air Fryer you choose will mostly depend on your available kitchen space.

Here is a list of some of the best Air Fryer manufacturers right now:

- Cosori
- Ninja
- Breville
- Philips
- Salter
- Teffal

You should also try to read the comments from previous users if you are thinking about buying a specific model.

the Year of Healthy Fried Foods

Are Air Fryers an expensive kitchen tool?

If we compare an Air Fryer to a conventional oven, then this tool is super economical to have in your kitchen. A good Air Fryer will cost somewhere between $100 to $250 USD.

If you are a shopping expert and savvy with sales, then of course you may find an even cheaper Air Fryer.

Is the food cooked in the Air Fryer healthier than deep-frying?

Air Fryer recipes are basically all updated deep-fried recipes that previously required a lot of oil. Air-fried food is thus generally more healthy than deep-fried food, as they have less calories and trans fats.

What type of food can I prepare in my Air Fryer?

Air Fryer technology is constantly developing, as are the tools you can buy for your Air Fryer basket. As a result, you can cook almost any type of dish, especially if you invest in a range of cooking pans and silicone moulds.

- Some suggested meal types:
- Air-fried snacks
- Main dishes featuring meat and fish
- Vegan dishes
- Toast and sandwiches
- Baked goods
- Desserts
- Snacks
- Veggies
- Stews
- Pasta
- Pizza

UNITS THAT WILL HELP YOU IN THE COOKING PROCESS

Cups	Liquids (ml)	Tablespoon (tbsp)	Tespoon (tsp)	Gram (g)	Ounces (Oz)
1/4	61	4	12	57	2
1/2	125	8	24	114	4
1/3	80	5tbsp+1tsp	16	76	2.6
1	250	16	48	227	8
			1/2	2.5	0.088
			1/4	1.25	0.044
				100	3.5
				200	7

Here is a conversion table for Fahrenheit and Celsius cooking temperatures:

Fahrenheit (F)	Celsius (C)
240	120
280	140
300	150
320	160
360	180
380	190
400	200

2 | SALTY STARTERS

1. Crispy curcuma onions
2. Salty popcorn with butter
3. Crunchy potato chips
4. Original zucchini chips
5. Yummy avocado sticks
6. Carrot chips
7. Crunchy bacon wrapped crackers
8. Small and crispy pork sausages
9. Cheesy asparagus spears
10. Smashed small potatoes
11. BBQ chicken wings
12. Stuffed cherry peppers with mozzarella
13. Cheese ball snacks
14. Focaccia snacks
15. Eggplant crisps
16. Calamari slices
17. Crispy sesame chicken sticks
18. Beef taquitos in corn tortillas
19. Parmesan cauliflower snacks
20. Garlic shrimp
21. Crispy zucchini and egg pillows

DON'T FORGET TO GET THE

TOP RECIPES FROM THIS BOOK AS

A DOWNLOADABLE PDF IN COLOUR

FOR FREE!

SCAN THE QR CODE BELOW

CRISPY CURCUMA ONIONS

These crispy onions rings will be a welcome dish at your next catch up with friends.

Serving size: 4 mini portions

TOTAL CALORIES: 61
Fat: 2g | Carbs: 10g | Protein: 1g

INGREDIENTS

- 2 large (or 3 medium) sized onions
- 1 tbsp. cooking oil
- A pinch of salt
- A pinch of pepper
- 1 tsp. curcuma

INSTRUCTIONS

1. Cut the onions into thinly sliced rings. Separate them from one another.
2. Preheat the Air Fryer to 160°C/320°F and add little oil to the cooking tray.
3. Mix the onion rings, spices and rest of the oil in a bowl.
4. Place the onions in the Air Fryer and bake them for 20 minutes. Lower the temperature to 100°C/200°F and continue cooking for a further 10 minutes.

SALTY POPCORN WITH BUTTER

Who doesn't love popcorn? It's a healthy and tasty snack that can easily be prepared in an Air Fryer.

Serving size: 2 portions

TOTAL CALORIES: 120
Fat: 7g | Carbs: 13g | Protein: 2g

INGREDIENTS

- 1/3 cup popcorn kernels
- 1 tbsp. butter
- 1 tsp. salt
- A pinch of curry, to taste

INSTRUCTIONS

1. Preheat the Air Fryer to 190°C/380°F.
2. Mix the corn kernels, butter, salt and curry in a bowl.
3. Add the mixture to the Air Fryer in a thin layer. Bake for 8 minutes, while shaking the basket every 2 minutes.
4. When you can no longer hear corn popping, it's ready.

CRUNCHY POTATO CHIPS

There's nothing better than chips without trans fats – so go for it!

Serving size: 1 portion

TOTAL CALORIES: 170
Fat: 2g | Carbs: 40g | Protein: 2g

INGREDIENTS

- 1 medium or large sticky potato (with a soft peel)
- A little oil for the cooking basket
- Salt
- Oregano or other spices to taste

INSTRUCTIONS

1. Preheat your Air Fryer to 190°C/380°F.
2. You can choose whether to peel the potato, keeping the skin is fine. Cut the potato into very thin slices, then use a soft napkin to dry the potato.
3. Place all the potatoes in a bowl and mix in the salt and spices.
4. Add a little oil to the basket. Then, add the potatoes and cook for 15 minutes. Shake the basket occasionally to prevent the chips from sticking. Enjoy!

ORIGINAL ZUCCHINI CHIPS

Zucchini chips might look tricky, but not with this recipe!

Serving size: 2 portions

TOTAL CALORIES: 40
Fat: 2g | Carbs: 5g | Protein: 0g

INGREDIENTS

- 1 medium sized zucchini
- A pinch of salt
- A little oil for the cooking basket

INSTRUCTIONS

1. Preheat your Air Fryer to 180°C/360°F.
2. Cut the zucchini into very thin circular pieces. Add them to a bowl and mix in the salt.
3. Add a little oil to the cooking basket, then add the zucchini. Cook for 30 minutes, shaking the basket every 10 minutes.

YUMMY AVOCADO STICKS

This recipe results in a tasty, crunchy avocado snack – demonstrating that traditionally creamy foods can also be crunchy.

Serving size: 2 portions

TOTAL CALORIES: 139
Fat: 4g | Carbs: 30g | Protein: 4g

iNGREDiENTS

- 1 avocado
- 1 egg
- ½ cup breadcrumbs

iNSTRUCTiONS

1. Preheat your Air Fryer to 190°C/380°F.
2. Cut the avocado in half, then into sticks that are half a centimetre thick. Beat the egg in a bowl.
3. Take one avocado stick and coat it in the beaten egg mixture, then toss it in the breadcrumbs. Repeat the process with all sticks.
4. Place the sticks in the Air Fryer and cook for 5 minutes. Turn them over and cook for a further 5 minutes.

CARROT CHIPS

Carrots are the perfect snack for your next gathering – don't skip this recipe!

Serving size: 2 portions

TOTAL CALORIES: 130
Fat: 2g | Carbs: 30g | Protein: 1g

iNGREDiENTS

- 4 medium (or 3 large) carrots
- A pinch of salt
- Oregano, to taste
- A little oil for the cooking basket

iNSTRUCTiONS

1. Preheat your Air Fryer to 175°C/350°F.
2. Cut the carrots into long sticks. Place them in a bowl and toss with the salt and oregano.
3. Add a little oil to the basket, then add the carrots and bake for 30 minutes.

7 CRUNCHY BACON WRAPPED CRACKERS

Imagine: thin crackers wrapped in crunchy bacon. Delicious.

Serving size: 3 portions

TOTAL CALORIES: 386
Fat: 16g | Carbs: 40g | Protein: 20g

INGREDIENTS

- 15 Stick crackers
- 15 thin pcs. of bacon
- A little oil for the cooking basket

INSTRUCTIONS

1. Preheat your Air Fryer to 190°C/380°F.
2. Wrap a piece of bacon around a stick, then repeat for all sticks.
3. Add a little oil to the basket, then place the sticks in the basket and bake for max. 10 minutes.

8 SMALL AND CRISPY PORK SAUSAGES

Snack sausages alongside your glass of beer? Perfect

Serving size: 3 portions

TOTAL CALORIES: 276
Fat: 20g | Carbs: 4g | Protein: 14G

INGREDIENTS

- 9-10 small pork sausages
- 2 tbsp. Tomato paste
- A pinch of salt
- Pepper
- A little oil for the cooking basket

INSTRUCTIONS

1. Preheat your Air Fryer to 190°C/380°F.
2. Make small cuts in the sausages then add them to a bowl and toss wish with tomato paste, salt and pepper.
3. Add a little oil to the basket, then add the sausages and cook for 5 minutes on each side.

CHEESY ASPARA-GUS SPEARS

This one is for the baked cheese and egg lovers. Enjoy this mouth-watering cheesy asparagus snack.

Serving size: 3 portions

TOTAL CALORIES: 150
Fat: 9g | Carbs: 4g | Protein: 7g

INGREDIENTS

- 10 asparagus spears
- 1 egg
- ½ cup grated cheddar cheese
- A pinch of salt
- A little oil for the cooking basket

INSTRUCTIONS

1. Preheat your Air Fryer to 160°C/320°F.
2. Mix the egg with the cheese, salt, then set the mixture aside.
3. Add a little oil to the basket, then add the asparagus spears and bake for 5 minutes.
4. Open the basket and pour the mixture of cheese over the asparagus spears. Bake for a further 7 minutes.
5. Take the asparagus out of the basket and separate the spears.

SMASHED SMALL POTATOES

You'll need a small glass for smashing the potatoes in this recipe, and they're so deliciously crunchy it's best to prepare as many as possible!

Serving size: 3 portions

TOTAL CALORIES: 310
Fat: 4g | Carbs: 67g | Protein: 3g

INGREDIENTS

- 2 cups small young potatoes
- 1 tbsp. butter
- Salt
- A pinch of pepper
- A little oil for the cooking basket

INSTRUCTIONS

1. Boil the potatoes with the peels on, for 15 minutes. Remove them from the water, then smash them with a glass.
2. Add a little oil to the basket, then add the potatoes to the basket, spreading them out in one layer. Add a little butter, salt and pepper to the top of every potato.
3. Cook the potatoes at 180°C/360°F for 15 minutes, checking on them once or twice.

BBQ CHICKEN WINGS

(IN MINUTES)
PREP
5
COOK
20

You'll be the favourite in your crew with this ultimate beer night snack.

Serving size: 4 portions

TOTAL CALORIES: 250
Fat: 17g | Carbs: 2g | Protein: 22g

INGREDIENTS

- 12-14 chicken wings
- A little oil for the cooking basket
- A pinch of salt
- 2 tbsp. BBQ sauce

INSTRUCTIONS

1. Preheat your Air Fryer to 190°C/380°F.
2. Add a little oil to the basket, then toss the chicken wings with some salt and add them to the basket. Bake for 20 minutes, shaking once.
3. Remove the chicken wings and place them in a bowl. Add the BBQ sauce and toss together.

STUFFED CHERRY PEPPERS WITH MOZZARELLA

(IN MINUTES)
PREP
10
COOK
15

For when you want some colour in your dish.

Serving size: 3 portions

TOTAL CALORIES: 140
Fat: 9g | Carbs: 2g | Protein: 10g

INGREDIENTS

- 10 small cherry peppers, multiple colours
- 150g/5.2oz mozzarella
- Chilli powder
- Salt
- A little oil for the cooking basket

INSTRUCTIONS

1. Slice the peppers in half and stuff them with mozzarella cheese. Sprinkle with salt and chilli powder.
2. Add a little oil to the basket, then add the peppers and bake for 15 minutes at 170°C/350°F.
3. Serve with little tzatziki sauce and enjoy.

CHEESE BALL SNACKS

A creamy and tasty snack.

Serving size: 4 portions

TOTAL CALORIES: 358
Fat: 18g | Carbs: 35g | Protein: 8g

INGREDIENTS

- 450g/15.8oz cheese balls (one bag of frozen cheese balls)
- 1/3 cup sriracha sauce
- A little oil for the cooking basket

INSTRUCTIONS

1. Preheat your Air Fryer to 190°C/380°F.
2. Add a little oil to the basket, then lay out the cheese balls in the basket in a single layer and cook for 15 minutes. Halfway through, open the Air Fryer and spray a little oil on the balls (it will make them crispier).
3. Serve with sriracha sauce and enjoy.

FOCACCIA SNACKS

Not quite a snack, not quite a meal, this focaccia will keep you full for longer when you prepare and serve it in small bites.

Serving size: 3 portions

TOTAL CALORIES: 220
Fat: 14g | Carbs: 20g | Protein: 10g

INGREDIENTS

- 3 pcs. old bread
- 2 tbsp. olive oil
- ½ cup cheddar cheese
- Fresh basil leaves
- 3 tbsp. tomato sauce

INSTRUCTIONS

1. Cut each piece of bread into four equal square pieces. Add little oil, tomato sauce, cheddar cheese and basil leaves to each piece of bread.
2. Preheat the Air Fryer to 175°C/350°F. Add a little oil to the basket.
3. Add the bread and bake for 10 minutes. Remove from the Air Fryer, serve and enjoy.

EGGPLANT CRISPS

Salty, meaty and crispy chips, these should be served with tasty dips and appetizers.

Serving size: 3 portions

TOTAL CALORIES: 154
Fat: 4g | Carbs: 22g | Protein: 6g

INGREDIENTS

- 2 eggs
- 1 eggplant
- ½ cup breadcrumbs
- 1 tsp. curry powder
- A little oil for the cooking basket
- Salt

INSTRUCTIONS

1. Cut the eggplant into very thin slices.
2. In a bowl, whisk the eggs, adding a little salt. In another bowl, mix the bread-crumbs with the curry powder.
3. Dip one slice of eggplant in the egg mixture, then with the breadcrumbs.
4. Add a little oil to the basket, then add one layer of the eggplant chips and bake for 5 minutes on each side. The temperature should be 180°C/360°F.

CALAMARI SLICES

Add a little mustard and you'll never get enough of this hot and tasty starter dish.

Serving size: 4 portions

TOTAL CALORIES: 125
Fat: 4g | Carbs: 12g | Protein: 11g

INGREDIENTS

- 200g/7oz calamari rings
- 3 tbsp. flour
- 1 tsp. oregano
- Salt
- 3 tbsp. breadcrumbs
- ¼ cup milk
- 1 egg
- A little oil for the cooking basket

INSTRUCTIONS

1. Mix the milk and egg in one bowl. Mix the oregano, flour and salt in another bowl. Mix the breadcrumbs and a little salt in a third bowl.
2. Take one calamari ring and toss it in the dish with flour, then toss it in the dish with milk and egg. Then, toss it in the dish with the breadcrumbs.
3. Add a little oil to the basket, then place the calamari rings in the Air Fryer in one layer.
4. Bake the calamari at 200°C/400°F for 5 minutes on each side.

CRISPY SESAME CHICKEN STICKS

These versatile sticks can be made spicy or salty, and you can serve them plain or add your favourite sauce.

Serving size: 3 portions

TOTAL CALORIES: 210
Fat: 6g | Carbs: 11g | Protein: 30g

INGREDIENTS

- 300g/10.5oz white chicken breast
- 2 tbsp. sesame seeds
- 1 egg
- 4 tbsp. breadcrumbs
- A little oil for the cooking basket

INSTRUCTIONS

1. Preheat your Air Fryer to 180°C/360°F.
2. Cut the chicken breast into thin slices no more than 2cm thick.
3. Whisk the egg in one bowl. In another bowl, mix the breadcrumbs with the sesame seeds and salt.
4. Take one chicken piece and dip it in the egg mixture, then toss with the breadcrumbs. Repeat the process for all chicken pieces.
5. Add a little oil to the basket, then add the chicken pieces and bake for 7 minutes on each side. Serve and enjoy.

BEEF TAQUITOS IN CORN TORTILLAS

Cooked without oil, these crispy tortillas will be your next favourite snack.

Serving size: 4 portions

TOTAL CALORIES: 260
Fat: 14g | Carbs: 12g | Protein: 16g

INGREDIENTS

- 16 store-bought beef taquitos in corn tortillas
- A little oil for the cooking basket

INSTRUCTIONS

1. Preheat your Air Fryer to 200°C/400°F.
2. Add a little oil to the basket.
3. Add the taquitos to the basket and bake for 5 minutes on each side. Serve and enjoy.

PARMESAN CAULI-FLOWER SNACKS

Yes, even cauliflower can be a tasty snack option!

Serving size: 2 portions

TOTAL CALORIES: 124

Fat: 5g | Carbs: 12g | Protein: 8g

INGREDIENTS

- 200g/7oz cauliflower
- 1 egg
- 1 tsp. red chilli pepper
- 4 tbsp. grated parmesan
- A little oil for the cooking basket

INSTRUCTIONS

1. Preheat your Air Fryer to 200°C/400°F.
2. Cut the cauliflower into small florets. Mix the parmesan, cauliflower and egg in a bowl.
3. Add a little oil to the basket, then add the cauliflower and bake for 15 minutes, shaking the basket twice throughout.

GARLIC SHRIMP

The perfect snack for a wine night or paired with a summer risotto.

Serving size: 4 portions

TOTAL CALORIES: 95

Fat: 4g | Carbs: 3g | Protein: 14g

INGREDIENTS

- 20 small shrimp
- ½ tsp. garlic powder
- ½ tsp. salt
- 2 tbsp. tomato paste
- A little oil for the cooking basket

INSTRUCTIONS

1. Preheat your Air Fryer to 200°C/400°F.
2. Mix the shrimp, tomato paste, salt and garlic together in a bowl.
3. Add a little oil to the basket, then add the shrimp and bake for 7 minutes on each side.

CRISPY ZUCCHINI AND EGG PILLOWS

This recipe is creamy on the inside and crispy on the outside – you won't be able to stop yourself!

Serving size: 3 portions

TOTAL CALORIES: 87

Fat: 4g | Carbs: 3g | Protein: 9g

INGREDIENTS

- 2 eggs
- ½ zucchini
- 3 tbsp. cottage cheese
- 2 tbsp. oat flour
- A pinch of salt
- A little oil for the cooking basket

INSTRUCTIONS

1. Preheat your Air Fryer to 160°C/320°F.
2. Grate the zucchini and place it in a bowl. Toss it with the egg, oat flour, cottage cheese and salt.
3. Line the basket with aluminium foil. Using a spoon, place small scoops of the zucchini mixture in the basket.
4. Bake for 15-20 minutes, frequently checking and turning the zucchini pillows.

3 | SNACKS

1. Toast sticks
2. Goat cheese with honey and sesame
3. Roasted seed mix
4. Kale and bacon chips
5. Roasted almonds
6. Mixed nut snacks

DON'T FORGET TO GET THE

TOP RECIPES FROM THIS BOOK AS

A DOWNLOADABLE PDF IN COLOUR

FOR FREE!

SCAN THE QR CODE BELOW

1 TOAST STICKS

A tasty and fulfilling snack.

Serving size: 3 portions

TOTAL CALORIES: 200

Fat: 9g | Carbs: 32g | Protein: 7g

INGREDIENTS

- 3 pcs. of bread
- 3 pcs. yellow cheese
- Butter, for spreading
- 1 tbsp. sesame seeds
- 3 tbsp. hummus
- A little oil for the cooking basket

INSTRUCTIONS

1. Step 1: Preheat your Air Fryer to 200°C/400°F.
2. Spread butter on every piece of bread, then add hummus and a slice of cheese. Cut the bread into three pieces. There will be a total of nine pieces.
3. Add a little oil to the basket, then place all bread pieces in the Air Fryer and sprinkle with sesame seeds.
4. Cook for 10 minutes. Serve and enjoy.

GOAT CHEESE WITH HONEY AND SESAME 2

This snack combines salty and sweet flavours – try it for a unique experience.

Serving size: 4 portions

TOTAL CALORIES: 186

Fat: 11g | Carbs: 9g | Protein: 10g

INGREDIENTS

- 200g/7oz goat cheese
- 2 tbsp. honey
- 2 tbsp. sesame seeds
- Rosemary, to taste
- A little oil for the cooking basket

INSTRUCTIONS

1. Preheat your Air Fryer to 180°C/360°F.
2. Cut the cheese into long strips, then place them on a flat surface and spread honey on every side of the cheese.
3. Add a little oil to the basket, then add the cheese sticks and spread the sesame and rosemary over them. Cook for 10 minutes. Serve and enjoy.

3. ROASTED SEED MIX

(IN MINUTES)
PREP 5
COOK 10

Seeds are a source of healthy fats and are very tasty once baked.

Serving size: 3 portions

TOTAL CALORIES: 360
Fat: 33g | Carbs: 8g | Protein: 10g

INGREDIENTS

- ¼ cup sunflower seeds
- ½ cup pumpkin seeds
- 1 tbsp. olive oil
- ½ tsp. salt
- ½ tsp. chilli powder

INSTRUCTIONS

1. Preheat your Air Fryer to 200°C/400°F.
2. Mix the seeds, spices and oil together.
3. Add baking paper to the basket and place the seed mixture inside. Cook for 12 minutes, shaking twice. Enjoy.

KALE AND BACON CHIPS 4.

(IN MINUTES)
PREP 5
COOK 10

Chips don't always need to come from potatoes! These low-carb chips can be perfectly prepared in an Air Fryer.

Serving size: 2 portions

TOTAL CALORIES: 160
Fat: 15g | Carbs: 1g | Protein: 9g

INGREDIENTS

- 4 kale leaves
- 4 slices bacon
- A little oil for the cooking basket
- Salt, to taste

INSTRUCTIONS

1. Preheat your Air Fryer to 180°C/360°F.
2. Cut the leaves of the kale from the spine. Slice the bacon into large pieces and toss with a little salt and oil.
3. Place the kale and bacon in the basket and bake for 10 minutes. If the bacon is too soft for your taste, bake for a further 2 minutes. Serve and enjoy.

ROASTED ALMONDS

Almonds are rich in Vitamin E and can be ready in minutes and taken anywhere.

Serving size: 3 portions

TOTAL CALORIES: 450

Fat: 38g | Carbs: 14g | Protein: 13g

INGREDIENTS

- 1 cup almonds
- 2 tbsp. water
- A pinch of various seasonings (curry, chilli, ginger, garlic powder)
- ½ tsp. salt

INSTRUCTIONS

1. Preheat your Air Fryer to 180°C/360°F.
2. In a bowl, mix the almonds, seasoning, water and salt together.
3. Place them in the Air Fryer basket and bake for 12 minutes, shaking constantly. Serve and enjoy.

MIXED NUT SNACKS

Mix your favourite nuts for a healthy Air Fryer snack!

Serving size: 3 portions

TOTAL CALORIES: 456

Fat: 42g | Carbs: 13g | Protein: 12g

INGREDIENTS

- ¼ cup hazelnuts
- ¼ cup walnuts
- ¼ cup cashews
- ¼ cup pistachios
- 2 tbsp. water
- ½ tsp. salt

INSTRUCTIONS

1. Preheat your Air Fryer to 180°C/360°F.
2. Mix all ingredients together in a bowl.
3. Place the mixture in the Air Fryer basket and bake for 12 minutes, shaking constantly. Serve and enjoy.

4 | SIDE DISHES

1. Cheesy baked kale
2. Crunchy green beans with chilli
3. Cheesy crunchy broccoli
4. Black sesame baby carrots
5. Mixed vegetables
6. Stuffed mushrooms
7. Caramelized crunchy beetroot
8. Bacon-stuffed whole baked potatoes
9. Mozzarella brussels sprouts
10. Pumpkin fries
11. Mixed Greek veggies
12. Seasoned butter bread
13. Roasted chickpeas with mushrooms
14. Kubeti salad
15. Chilli plantains
16. Potato latkes with egg
17. Sweet potato slices with mozzarella & tomato
18. Scandinavian veggie mix
19. Classic grilled mushrooms
20. Garlic pita bread with rosemary
21. Pesto pastry twists
22. Black beans with scallions

DON'T FORGET TO GET THE

TOP RECIPES FROM THIS BOOK AS

A DOWNLOADABLE PDF IN COLOUR

FOR FREE!

SCAN THE QR CODE BELOW

CHEESY BAKED KALE

A quick side dish for a meat or fish main.

Serving size: 4 portions

(IN MINUTES)
PREP
5
COOK
10

TOTAL CALORIES: 67

Fat: 4g | Carbs: 2g | Protein: 4g

INGREDIENTS

- 200g/7oz fresh kale
- 1/3 cup chopped white onion
- ½ cup cheddar cheese, grated
- A pinch of black pepper
- ½ tsp. salt

INSTRUCTIONS

1. Preheat your Air Fryer to 200°C/400°F.
2. Cut the kale into very small pieces. In a bowl, mix the kale, cheddar cheese, white onion, black pepper and salt.
3. Add a little oil to the basket, then add the mixture to the basket and bake for 10 minutes. Serve and enjoy.

CRUNCHY GREEN BEANS WITH CHILLI

(IN MINUTES)
PREP
2
COOK
10

Beans are a great source of protein and fibre, so this dish is a healthy choice as well as a tasty choice.

Serving size: 4 portions

TOTAL CALORIES: 185

Fat: 2.5g | Carbs: 35g | Protein: 6g

INGREDIENTS

- 300g/10.5oz green steamed peas
- 1 small carrot, cut into small pieces
- 1 tbsp. sriracha
- 1 small jalapeno pepper, diced
- A pinch of salt
- 1 tsp. honey
- A little oil for the cooking basket

INSTRUCTIONS

1. Preheat your Air Fryer to 160°C/320°F.
2. In a bowl, mix the beans, carrot, sriracha, jalapeno pepper, salt and honey.
3. Add a little oil to the basket, then add the beans and bake them for 10 minutes.

CHEESY CRUNCHY BROCCOLI

Broccoli isn't always popular with children, but this is one recipe that will convince them otherwise!

Serving size: 3 portions

TOTAL CALORIES: 92

Fat: 3g | Carbs: 13g | Protein: 5g

INGREDIENTS

- 300g/10.5oz broccoli
- 3 slices American cheese
- A pinch of salt
- A little oil for the cooking basket
- 1 tbsp. Mexican sauce

INSTRUCTIONS

1. Preheat your Air Fryer to 180°C/360°F.
2. Cut the broccoli into small pieces. Add it to a bowl and combine with the sauce and salt.
3. Add a little oil to the basket, then add the broccoli mixture and cover it with American cheese.
4. Bake for 15 minutes. Serve and enjoy.

BLACK SESAME BABY CARROTS

Carrots are high in beta-carotene, and they're a tasty side dish that can be quickly prepared.

Serving size: 4 portions

TOTAL CALORIES: 99

Fat: 6g | Carbs: 8g | Protein: 3g

INGREDIENTS

- 300g baby carrots
- 2tbsp. black sesame
- 1 tbsp. olive oil
- Salt, to taste

INSTRUCTIONS

1. Preheat your Air Fryer to 180°C/360°F.
2. In a bowl, combine the baby carrots, black sesame, salt and oil.
3. Add aluminium foil to the basket. Add the carrot mixture and cook for 20 minutes, checking once or twice throughout. Serve and enjoy.

MIXED VEGETABLES

STUFFED MUSHROOMS

Vegetables can be added to any main dish!

Serving size: 3 portions

A stunning side dish for a truly luxurious dinner.

Serving size: 2 portions

TOTAL CALORIES: 124
Fat: 10g | Carbs: 8g | Protein: 2g

TOTAL CALORIES: 156
Fat: 12g | Carbs: 4g | Protein: 10g

INGREDIENTS

- ½ cup cauliflower
- ½ cup broccoli
- ½ cup carrots
- 10 brussels sprouts
- 2 tbsp. olive oil
- Salt and pepper, to taste

INGREDIENTS

- 16 small white mushrooms
- 2 green peppers
- ½ cup grated parmesan
- A pinch of black pepper
- Salt, to taste
- A little oil for the cooking basket

INSTRUCTIONS

1. Preheat your Air Fryer to 200°C/400°F.
2. Cut the veggies to a size that is convenient for you. Toss them with salt and oil.
3. Add baking paper to the basket and add the veggies. Bake for 10 minutes, then shake once and bake for another 5 minutes if you'd like a crispier finish. Serve and enjoy.

INSTRUCTIONS

1. Preheat your Air Fryer to 170°C/340°F.
2. Cut the stems from the mushrooms. Dice the green pepper into small pieces, then fill the mushrooms with the peppers and grated parmesan.
3. Add a little oil to the basket, then add the mushrooms in a single layer. Bake for 15 minutes, checking once. Serve and enjoy.

THE AIR FRYER COOKBOOK FOR BEGINNERS

CARAMELIZED CRUNCHY BEET-ROOT

Beetroot supports healthy blood and the normal function of your gastrointestinal tract. In this recipe, you'll hardly believe beetroot is involved!

Serving size: 4 servings

TOTAL CALORIES: 60
Fat: 1.2g | Carbs: 12g | Protein: 1g

INGREDIENTS

- 3 small beetroots (the size of your palm)
- 1 tbsp. honey
- 1 tsp. salt
- 1 tsp. red chilli pepper
- A little oil for the cooking basket

INSTRUCTIONS

1. Preheat your Air Fryer to 160°C/320°F.
2. Slices the beetroot, then add them to a bowl and combine with the honey, salt and red chilli pepper.
3. Add a little oil to the basket, then add the beetroot in a single layer – if you have more beetroot left in the bowl, cook it in separate batches. Bake for 20 minutes. Check whether the beetroot is crispy and bake for a further 5 minutes if not. Serve and enjoy.

BACON-STUFFED WHOLE BAKED POTATOES

Bacon and potatoes are an excellent combination. In this recipe soft and creamy potato is paired with crunchy bacon.

Serving size: 4 portions

TOTAL CALORIES: 344
Fat: 20g | Carbs: 34g | Protein: 4g

INGREDIENTS

- 4 large young potatoes
- 8 tsp. butter
- Garlic powder, to taste
- 4 slices bacon
- A little oil for the cooking basket
- Curry powder, to taste

INSTRUCTIONS

1. Preheat your Air Fryer to 180°C/360°F.
2. You don't have to peel the potatoes, just scrub them well. Cut them in half and scoop deep holes from the centre.
3. Chop the bacon into very small pieces. Add one tsp. butter to the hole in each potato, then add bacon.
4. Add a little oil to the basket, then add the potatoes and bake for 30 minutes, checking them once or twice throughout. Enjoy.

MOZZARELLA BRUSSELS SPROUTS

This easy recipe has only a few ingredients, but the end result is pure garnish perfection.

Serving size: 3 portions

TOTAL CALORIES: 125
Fat: 6g | Carbs: 9g | Protein: 7g

INGREDIENTS

- 300g/10.5oz brussels sprouts
- ½ cup mozzarella, grated
- Salt and pepper, to taste
- A little oil for the cooking basket

INSTRUCTIONS

1. Preheat your Air Fryer to 170°C/340°F.
2. Cut the brussels sprouts in half.
3. Add a little oil to the basket, then add the brussels sprouts and cover them with mozzarella. Add a little salt.
4. Bake for 20 minutes, checking on them once. Enjoy.

PUMPKIN FRIES

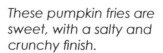

These pumpkin fries are sweet, with a salty and crunchy finish.

Serving size: 3 portions

TOTAL CALORIES: 130
Fat: 10g | Carbs: 8g | Protein: 1g

INGREDIENTS

- 1 small pumpkin (approx. 400g/14.1oz)
- 2 tbsp. olive oil
- Salt, to taste

INSTRUCTIONS

1. Preheat your Air Fryer to 200°C/400°F.
2. Cut the pumpkin into 'French fries'. Toss them with the oil and salt.
3. Add the pumpkin to the basket (in two separate batches) and bake for 20 minutes, shaking the basket once or twice throughout. Enjoy.

MIXED GREEK VEGGIES

An easy Mediterranean-inspired dish that will treat all your senses.

Serving size: 3 portions

TOTAL CALORIES: 60
Fat: 1.5g | Carbs: 6g | Protein: 1.5g

INGREDIENTS

- 1 red pepper
- ½ zucchini
- ½ eggplant
- 1 carrot
- 5 cherry tomatoes
- 1 small purple onion
- A little oil for the cooking basket
- A pinch of oregano
- A pinch of salt

INSTRUCTIONS

1. Preheat your Air Fryer to 160°C/320°F.
2. Cut all the vegetables into cubes (except the tomatoes). Combine them with the salt and oregano.
3. Add a little oil to the basket, then add the veggies and bake for 15 minutes, shaking the basket once or twice throughout. Serve and enjoy.

SEASONED BUTTER BREAD

This is the perfect side dish for a sauce-based meat recipe.

Serving size: 4 portions

TOTAL CALORIES: 346
Fat: 24.5g | Carbs: 2.7g | Protein: 28g
Sugar: 1.4g | Fibre: 0.4g

INGREDIENTS

- 4 thin slices sourdough bread
- 4 tsp. butter
- Garlic powder, to taste
- Mixed spice seasoning (oregano, rosemary, parsley)
- A little oil for the cooking basket

INSTRUCTIONS

1. Preheat your Air Fryer to 200°C/400°F.
2. Spread butter over every slice of bread, on both sides. Season the bread, sprinkling a little garlic and salt over each side.
3. Add a little oil to the basket, then add the bread and bake it on each side for 5 minutes. Serve and enjoy.

ROASTED CHICKPEAS WITH MUSHROOMS

Crunchy and fulfilling, chickpeas can be cooked in a variety of different ways – and this recipe is a must.

Serving size: 4 portions

TOTAL CALORIES: 80
Fat: 3.5g | Carbs: 9g | Protein: 3g

INGREDIENTS

- 200g/7oz canned chickpeas
- 5-6 medium sized white mushrooms
- 1 tbsp. olive oil
- ½ tsp. salt
- ½ tsp. curry spice

INSTRUCTIONS

1. Preheat your Air Fryer to 200°C/400°F.
2. Slice the mushrooms into extra thin slices. Combine the mushrooms, chickpeas, curry, olive oil and salt.
3. Add the mixture to the basket and cook for 20 minutes, opening once or twice to shake the basket.

KUBETI SALAD

This salad is a must for your next family gathering. Serve it in a large bowl and admire the colours.

Serving size: 4 portions

TOTAL CALORIES: 123
Fat: 5g | Carbs: 16g | Protein: 2.5g

INGREDIENTS

- 4 slices bread
- 2 tomatoes
- 1 cucumber
- A handful of parsley
- 10 black olives
- 1 tbsp. olive oil
- Salt, to taste

INSTRUCTIONS

1. Preheat your Air Fryer to 200°C/400°F.
2. Cut the bread into very small cubes.
3. Add a little oil to the basket, then add the cubed bread and bake for 10 minutes.
4. Chop the veggies and place them in a bowl. When the bread cubes are ready, add them to the salad. Season with parsley, salt and olive oil. Don't forget to add the olives! Enjoy.

CHILLI PLANTAINS

(IN MINUTES)
PREP
5
COOK
20

Bananas are a traditional side dish in Mexican cuisine. With an Air Fryer, you can now prepare them without deep frying!

Serving size: 4 portions

TOTAL CALORIES: 78

Fat: 2g | Carbs: 15g | Protein: 1g

INGREDIENTS

- 2 young, green bananas
- 1 tsp. ground chilli powder
- 1 sliced jalapeno pepper
- 2 tbsp. breadcrumbs
- A little oil for the cooking basket
- A pinch of salt

INSTRUCTIONS

1. Preheat your Air Fryer to 180°C/360°F.
2. Cut the bananas into medium slices. Place them in a bowl and toss with the chilli pepper, breadcrumbs, sliced jalapeno and salt.
3. Add a little oil to the basket, then add the bananas and cook for 20 minutes, shaking the basket 2-3 times throughout.

POTATO LATKES WITH EGG

(IN MINUTES)
PREP
5
COOK
20

This is an unusual recipe that traditionally requires a lot of oil – but this Air Fryer version is not only healthier, it's tastier!

Serving size: 3 portions

TOTAL CALORIES: 113

Fat: 3.5g | Carbs: 18g | Protein: 3g

INGREDIENTS

- 2 medium sized potatoes
- 1 egg
- 1 small onion
- 2 tbsp. wheat flour
- ½ tsp. salt
- ½ tsp. chilli powder
- A little oil for the cooking basket

INSTRUCTIONS

1. Preheat your Air Fryer to 200°C/400°F.
2. Grate the onion and potatoes, then drain any excess water and add the mixture to a bowl. Combine with one egg, the flour, salt and chilli powder.
3. Add baking paper to the bottom of the Air Fryer basket. Add one spoonful of the mixture to the basket, and repeat, keeping each spoonful separate. The latkes that you are forming should have an irregular shape.
4. When the basket is full, cook for 10 minutes on each side. Serve and enjoy.

SWEET POTATO SLICES WITH MOZ-ZARELLA & TOMATO

Sweet potato is the oldest type of potato still in use by mankind. Its orange colouring is thanks to its beta-carotene content, and it is of high nutritional value.

Serving size: 4 portions

TOTAL CALORIES: 175
Fat: 9g | Carbs: 10g | Protein: 11g

INGREDIENTS

- 1 large sweet potato
- 2 medium tomatoes
- 2 small balls of mozzarella
- Salt, to taste
- Dried basil, to taste
- A little oil for the cooking basket

INSTRUCTIONS

1. Preheat your Air Fryer to 170°C/340°F.
2. Cut the potato into thick slices, then slice the tomato and mozzarella. Take one slice of potato, then place a slice of tomato and mozzarella on top. Sprinkle with a little basil and salt.
3. Add a little oil to the basket, then place the potato slices in the basket (if there isn't enough space for all of them, you can prepare them in separate batches).
4. Cook for 25 minutes, checking once or twice throughout. Serve and enjoy.

SCANDINAVIAN VEGGIE MIX

Scandinavia has a great culture of side dishes that are perfect to serve alongside a seafood dish.

Serving size: 3 portions

TOTAL CALORIES: 76
Fat: 4g | Carbs: 10g | Protein: 1g

INGREDIENTS

- 1 large onion
- 1 zucchini
- 1 potato
- Rosemary, to taste
- 1 tbsp. butter
- A pinch of salt

INSTRUCTIONS

1. Preheat your Air Fryer to 180°C/360°F.
2. Chop the veggies into big pieces. Toss them with salt and rosemary, then heat the butter and add it to the veggies and mix.
3. Add a little oil to the basket, then add the veggies and bake for 20 minutes, checking once throughout. Serve and enjoy.

CLASSIC GRILLED MUSHROOMS

(IN MINUTES)
PREP
5
COOK
15

Did you know that mushrooms come from mycelia, which is unique in its ability to never use the soil to grow, instead nourishing the soil and helping other plants to grow?

Serving size: 3 portions

TOTAL CALORIES: 56
Fat: 3g | Carbs: 3g | Protein: 3g

INGREDIENTS

- 400g/14.1oz mushroom
- Garlic powder, to taste
- A little salt
- A little melted butter

INSTRUCTIONS

1. Preheat your Air Fryer to 200°C/400°F.
2. Cut the mushrooms into very thin slices. Combine them with the melted butter, salt and garlic powder.
3. Add them to the Air Fryer basket and cook for 15 minutes. Serve and enjoy.

GARLIC PITA BREAD WITH ROSEMARY

(IN MINUTES)
PREP
5
COOK
7

Pita bread is the basis of many meals, from gyros to doner.

Serving size: 1 portion

TOTAL CALORIES: 287
Fat: 16g | Carbs: 28g | Protein: 6g

INGREDIENTS

- 1 frozen pita bread
- 1 tbsp. butter
- 1 clove garlic
- A little rosemary
- Salt, to taste

INSTRUCTIONS

1. Step 1: Preheat your Air Fryer to 200°C/400°F.
2. Step 2: Dice or grate the garlic. Melt the butter and combine it with the garlic and rosemary. Spread the butter mixture over the pita bread.
3. Step 3: Add the pita bread to the basket and bake for 5-7 minutes. Serve and enjoy.

PESTO PASTRY TWISTS

(IN MINUTES)
PREP
10
COOK
10

In this recipe pastry and pesto are combined in puffy, soft twists.

Serving size: 4 portions

TOTAL CALORIES: 290
Fat: 18g | Carbs: 29g | Protein: 1g

INGREDIENTS

- 1 piece frozen puff pastry
- 2 tbsp. pesto
- A little oil for the cooking basket

INSTRUCTIONS

1. Preheat your Air Fryer to 200°C/400°F.
2. Spread the pesto sauce over the pastry sheet. Slice the pastry into long strips. Take each strip and twist it, like a spiral.
3. Add a little oil to the basket, then add the twists and bake for 10 minutes.

BLACK BEANS WITH SCALLIONS

(IN MINUTES)
PREP
5
COOK
15

This Mexican-inspired recipe is a great side dish for a vegan falafel or vegetarian sausages.

Serving size: 4 portions

TOTAL CALORIES: 186
Fat: 8g | Carbs: 17g | Protein: 10g

INGREDIENTS

- 1 cup canned black beans
- 2 scallions
- 2 tbsp. olive oil
- 1 tbsp. tomato sauce
- ½ tsp. salt
- A pinch of black pepper

INSTRUCTIONS

1. Preheat your Air Fryer to 180°C/360°F.
2. Dice the scallions, then combine them with the beans, olive oil, salt, tomato sauce and black pepper.
3. Add the mixture to the basket and bake for 15 minutes, shaking the basket every now and then. Serve and enjoy.

5 | BAKED GOODS

1. Buttery air-fried biscuits
2. Raspberry muffins
3. Puffed triangles with pepperoni and yellow cheese
4. Air-fried chocolate cookies
5. Vanilla cannoli
6. Soft and crunchy doughnuts
7. Puffed pillows with cottage cheese
8. Cinnamon rolls
9. Vanilla cream toast sticks
10. Sugar-dusted beignets
11. Mini apple pies
12. Italian bread with olive oil
13. Hot homemade buns with dried cranberries
14. Traditional butter bagels
15. Mini oat pancakes
16. Gluten-free seeded bread
17. Small pumpkin bread balls
18. Bacon muffins with sour cream

DON'T FORGET TO GET THE

TOP RECIPES FROM THIS BOOK AS

A DOWNLOADABLE PDF IN COLOUR

FOR FREE!

SCAN THE QR CODE BELOW

BUTTERY AIR-FRIED BISCUITS

These biscuits are incredibly tasty alongside your morning coffee!

Serving size: 4 portions

TOTAL CALORIES: 224

Fat: 16g | Carbs: 10g | Protein: 9g

INGREDIENTS

- 1 pack refrigerated canned biscuits
- 1 tbsp. butter
- Cinnamon, to taste

INSTRUCTIONS

1. Preheat your Air Fryer to 200°C/400°F.
2. Melt the butter and spread it over every biscuit. Sprinkle the biscuits with a little cinnamon.
3. Place them in the basket and cook for 20 minutes.

RASPBERRY MUFFINS

No party is complete without muffins – they always bring joy and happiness.

Serving size: 4 portions

TOTAL CALORIES: 404

Fat: 15g | Carbs: 65g | Protein: 7.5g

INGREDIENTS

- 1 cup flour
- ¼ cup oil
- 2 eggs
- ½ cup sugar
- 1 cup raspberries
- 1 tbsp. baking soda
- 1 tbsp. vanilla sugar
- 4 silicon muffin pans

INSTRUCTIONS

1. Preheat your Air Fryer to 200°C/400°F.
2. Combine all the ingredients in a bowl, using a whisk to mix them well.
3. Fill each silicon muffin pan 2/3 full.
4. Place them in the Air Fryer and cook for 20-25 minutes. Serve and enjoy.

PUFFED TRIANGLES WITH PEPPERONI & YELLOW CHEESE

Small, crunchy triangles filled with melting cheese, served immediately after baking.

Serving size: 4 portions

TOTAL CALORIES: 412

Fat: 25g | Carbs: 31g | Protein: 11g

INGREDIENTS

- Frozen puff pastry sheets
- 100g/3.5oz pepperoni
- 100/3.5oz grated yellow cheese
- A small amount of oil
- 2 tbsp. sesame seeds

INSTRUCTIONS

1. Preheat your Air Fryer to 200°C/400°F.
2. Cut the puff pastry into squares. To each square add a little cheese and pepperoni, then fold the square in half to form a triangle.
3. Brush a little oil over each triangle then season with sesame seeds.
4. Place them in the Air Fryer basket and bake for 10 minutes. Serve and enjoy.

AIR-FRIED CHOCOLATE COOKIES

This chocolate cookie recipe is sweet, cocoa filled and always enjoyable.

Serving size: 4 portions

TOTAL CALORIES: 342

Fat: 10g | Carbs: 57g | Protein: 4g

INGREDIENTS

- ¾ cup flour
- 1 tbsp. raw cocoa
- 1/3 cup chocolate chips
- 1/3 cup sugar
- 1 tsp. baking soda
- 1 egg
- 2 tbsp. melted butter

INSTRUCTIONS

1. Preheat your Air Fryer to 180°C/360°F.
2. In a bowl, mix all the ingredients together. Then, using your hands, form small balls from the mixture.
3. Add a little oil to the basket, then add the balls while keeping them separate from each other (the cookies will grow). Bake for 20 minutes, then serve and enjoy.

VANILLA CANNOLI

Italian cannoli are traditionally deep-fried and served in small quantities. With this recipe and an Air Fryer, you can skip the trans fats for a fulfilling treat.

Serving size: 10 portions

TOTAL CALORIES: 153

Fat: 7.1g | Carbs: 13g | Protein: 7.2g

INGREDIENTS

For the shells:

- 1 cup all-purpose flour
- 3 tbsp. sugar
- ½ tsp. cinnamon
- ½ tsp. salt
- 3 tbsp. white wine
- 2 tbsp. butter
- 1 small egg

For the filling:

- 200g/7oz ricotta cheese
- 2 tbsp. mascarpone cheese
- 2 tbsp. sugar
- ½ cup heavy cream
- 1 stick of vanilla

INSTRUCTIONS

1. Combine all ingredients for the shells in a bowl. You can use your hands, or a hand mixer. Place the dough on a floured surface and roll it out thinly. Using a circular cutter, cut out the cannoli shapes. Wrap each piece of dough around a cannoli mould.
2. Preheat your Air Fryer to 140°C/360°F.
3. Add a little oil to the basket, then place the cannoli moulds in the basket and bake for 15 minutes, checking once throughout.
4. To prepare the filling, beat the heavy cream together with the sugar in a bowl. Add the rest of the ingredients to the mixture and combine with a hand mixer. Refrigerate the cream until you are ready to fill the cannoli.

SOFT AND CRUNCHY DOUGHNUTS

A morning with doughnuts is a perfect morning – especially if they aren't deep-fried!

Serving size: 4 portions

TOTAL CALORIES: 238

Fat: 10g | Carbs: 18g | Protein: 16g

INGREDIENTS

- 1 cup all-purpose flour
- ¼ cup milk
- 2 tbsp. sugar
- Salt, to taste
- 1 egg
- 1 stick vanilla
- 2 tbsp. melted butter
- ½ pack active, dry yeast

INSTRUCTIONS

1. Combine the milk with a little sugar and yeast. Let it rest for 10 minutes.
2. In a separate bowl, combine the rest of the ingredients. Then, add the milk mixture. Mix everything together until a dough is formed. Knead the dough on a floured surface, then leave it in a warm place for 1 hour to let it double in size.
3. Take the dough and place it on a newly floured surface. Roll it out thickly, and with a glass or circular cutter, cut out your doughnuts.
4. Leave the doughnuts in a warm place for 20 minutes.
5. Step 5: Preheat your Air Fryer to 170°C/340°F.
6. Add a little oil to the basket, then add the doughnuts and bake for 6-7 minutes.

THE AIR FRYER COOKBOOK FOR BEGINNERS

PUFFED PILLOWS WITH COTTAGE CHEESE

Perfect for weekend gatherings.

Serving size: 4 portions

TOTAL CALORIES: 336
Fat: 18g | Carbs: 31g | Protein: 7g

INGREDIENTS

- 1 sheet frozen puff pastry
- 4 tbsp. cottage cheese
- 1 egg white

INSTRUCTIONS

1. Preheat your Air Fryer to 200°C/400°F.
2. Cut 3cm squares from the puff pastry. To the middle of every square, add cottage cheese. Place another pastry square over the cottage cheese and seal the edges using a fork. Beat the egg white, then brush it over the pastry pillows.
3. Add a little oil to the basket, then add the pillows and cook for 10 minutes. Serve and enjoy.

CINNAMON ROLLS

This is an extra-quick recipe for cinnamon lovers.

Serving size: 4 portions

TOTAL CALORIES: 447
Fat: 23g | Carbs: 51g | Protein: 5g

INGREDIENTS

Ingredients:

- 1 sheet frozen puff pastry
- 2 tbsp. melted butter
- 1 tbsp. cinnamon
- 2 tbsp. sugar

For the glaze

- 3 tbsp. heavy cream
- 2 tbsp. normal milk
- 4 tbsp. powdered sugar

INSTRUCTIONS

1. Spread butter over the puff pastry sheet. Combine the sugar and cinnamon, then sprinkle it over the buttered pastry. Cut long strips from the pastry and use these to form rolls.
2. Preheat your Air Fryer to 200°C/400°F.
3. Add a little oil to the basket, then add the cinnamon rolls and bake for 10 minutes.
4. Whisk the heavy cream with a hand whisker, and slowly add the sugar and milk.
5. Take the cinnamon rolls out of the Air Fryer and brush a little of the glaze over every roll. Enjoy.

VANILLA CREAM TOAST STICKS

A sweet, soft, and cheesy toast-based breakfast.

Serving size: 2 portions

TOTAL CALORIES: 224
Fat: 5g | Carbs: 35g | Protein: 10g

INGREDIENTS

- 4 slices bread
- 2 tbsp. mascarpone cheese
- 4 tbsp. vanilla pudding
- A little butter

INSTRUCTIONS

1. Preheat your Air Fryer to 180°C/360°F.
2. Cut each slice of bread in half. Spread a little butter over the outer side of the bread. On the inner side of one slice of bread part spread mascarpone and on a second, spread vanilla cream. Unite the pieces together.
3. Add a little oil to the basket, then place the coated bread in the basket and bake for 15 minutes. Serve and enjoy.

SUGAR-DUSTED BEIGNETS

Traditionally, this French-inspired recipe requires deep-fried dough covered in powdered sugar. Skip the deep-frying with an Air Fryer and notice the difference.

Serving size: 4 portions

TOTAL CALORIES: 310
Fat: 12g | Carbs: 43g | Protein: 7g

INGREDIENTS

- 1 cup all-purpose flour
- 1 tbsp. sugar
- 1 mini pack of dried yeast
- 1 egg
- ½ cup heavy cream
- 2 tbsp. melted butter
- ¼ cup hot water
- Powdered sugar, for dusting

INSTRUCTIONS

1. In a bowl, combine all the ingredients (except the powdered sugar). Mix well with an automatic mixer. Knead the mixture on a floured surface for 5 minutes. Cover the dough with a blanket and leave it to chill in the fridge overnight.
2. Knead the dough again over a floured surface, then roll it out in a thick layer. Cut it into 2cm squares.
3. Preheat the Air Fryer to 170°C/350°F.
4. Add a little oil to the basket, then add the beignets and bake for 13-14 minutes. Dust with powdered sugar and enjoy.

MINI APPLE PIES

This quick apple pie recipe might be a little different from your grandmother's version, but it's definitely worth a try.

Serving size: 4 portions

TOTAL CALORIES: 378
Fat: 15g | Carbs: 52g | Protein: 4.5g

INGREDIENTS

- 1 sheet frozen puff pastry
- 2 green apples
- 3 tbsp. sugar
- Vanilla stick
- ½ tsp. cinnamon

INSTRUCTIONS

1. Grate the apples, then combine them with the cinnamon, sugar and vanilla.
2. Take a silicone mini pie mould and line the moulds with the puff pastry.
3. Fill the pastry with the apple mixture.
4. Preheat your Air Fryer to 200°C/400°F.
5. Place the mini pies in the Air Fryer and cook for 13-15 minutes, checking once. Serve and enjoy.

ITALIAN BREAD WITH OLIVE OIL

There's nothing better than the smell of baked bread in the morning. Add a slice of cheese or a tomato salad to this version.

Serving size: 5 portions

TOTAL CALORIES: 334
Fat: 8g | Carbs: 60g | Protein: 8g

INGREDIENTS

- 2 cups flour
- 2/3 cup water
- 2 tsp. salt
- 1 mini pack dried yeast
- 20ml olive oil
- Fresh oregano

INSTRUCTIONS

1. Combine the dried yeast with the water and salt. Add the flour and half of the olive oil. Knead the mixture well, then let it rest for 2 hours. Then, add a little more olive oil and knead the dough again.
2. Preheat your Air Fryer to 180°C/360°F.
3. Add baking paper and a little oil to the basket. Place the dough inside and make small indentations with your fingers. Sprinkle with oregano. Bake for 35-40 minutes.

HOT HOMEMADE BUNS WITH DRIED CRANBERRIES

(IN MINUTES)
PREP
180
COOK
20

This quick and easy recipe is a great choice for your child's lunch box.

Serving size: 4 portions

TOTAL CALORIES: 349

Fat: 8g | Carbs: 53g | Protein: 10g

INGREDIENTS

- 1 cup hot water
- 1 mini pack dried yeast
- 2 tbsp. sugar
- 2 tbsp. butter
- 3 tbsp. dried cranberries
- A little salt
- 2 cups flour

INSTRUCTIONS

1. Combine the warm water with yeast and 1 tbsp. sugar. Let the mixture bubble a little. Then, add the rest of the ingredients and begin to knead the dough. Continue until it a firm dough has formed (always keep a little flour aside in case your dough is very soft). When the dough is no longer sticky, shaped it into small balls. Place them in a pan and cover. Leave in a warm place for 2 hours.
2. Preheat your Air Fryer to 180°C/360°F.
3. Add baking paper to the basket, then add the buns. Bake for 20 minutes and serve. Enjoy.

TRADITIONAL BUTTER BAGELS

(IN MINUTES)
PREP
20
COOK
20

An alternative to your morning omelette or bowl of yoghurt, these bagels are an easy meal on the go.

Serving size: 4 portions

TOTAL CALORIES: 220

Fat: 8g | Carbs: 37g | Protein: 5g

INGREDIENTS

- 1 cup flour
- 1 mini pack of dried yeast
- A pinch of salt
- ½ cup hot water
- 2 tbsp. olive oil
- 1 tbsp. cumin

INSTRUCTIONS

1. Combine the hot water with the yeast and let it bubble a little. Add the flour, salt and olive oil. Knead the dough and then let it rest for 20 minutes.
2. Form small balls from the dough, then roll them out into thick 'sausages'. Form the bagels and sprinkle them with cumin.
3. Preheat your Air Fryer to 180°C/360°F.
4. Add baking paper to the basket, then add the bagels. Cook for 20 minutes. Serve and enjoy.

THE AIR FRYER COOKBOOK FOR BEGINNERS

MINI OAT PAN-CAKES

These pancakes can be served with anything you desire – from peanut butter to cocoa cream or fruit.

Serving size: 4 portions

TOTAL CALORIES: 220
Fat: 2g | Carbs: 44g | Protein: 8g

INGREDIENTS

- 1 cup rolled oats
- 1 banana
- 1 egg
- 3 tbsp. milk

INSTRUCTIONS

1. Preheat your Air Fryer to 200°C/400°F.
2. In a food blender, combine all the ingredients.
3. Add baking paper to the basket, then add the mixture as small pancakes. Cook for 5 minutes on each side.
4. Serve with cream and jam, and enjoy.

GLUTEN-FREE SEEDED BREAD

A tasty gluten-free bread recipe, this is destined to become a favourite.

Serving size: 6 portions

TOTAL CALORIES: 420
Fat: 26g | Carbs: 30g | Protein: 15g

INGREDIENTS

- 1 cup mixed seeds (flax, sesame, sunflower, chia, pumpkin)
- ½ cup gluten free oat flour (blended oats)
- 1 egg
- ½ cup water
- A pinch of salt

INSTRUCTIONS

1. Preheat your Air Fryer to 160°C/320°F.
2. Mix the ingredients together well.
3. Add baking paper to the basket and then add the seed mixture. Cook for 25-30 minutes, checking once or twice throughout. Serve and enjoy.

SMALL PUMPKIN BREAD BALLS

A great pumpkin-based autumn treat for all the family.

Serving size: 4 portions

TOTAL CALORIES: 317
Fat: 9g | Carbs: 50g | Protein: 6g

INGREDIENTS

- 1 cup pumpkin puree
- 1 cup flour
- 2 tbsp. sugar
- 1 egg
- ½ tsp. baking soda
- 2 tbsp. sunflower oil

INSTRUCTIONS

1. Preheat your Air Fryer to 200°C/400°F.
2. Mix all ingredients together until well combined. Take the silicon moulds and fill them until half full.
3. Place the moulds in the Air Fryer basket and bake for 20 minutes. Serve and enjoy.

BACON MUFFINS WITH SOUR CREAM

You can never have enough bacon in baked goods – and this recipe is the perfect bacon-filled snack.

Serving size: 4 portions

TOTAL CALORIES: 345
Fat: 15g | Carbs: 40g | Protein: 10g

INGREDIENTS

- 3 slices bacon
- 2 eggs
- 1 cup flour
- 2 tbsp. olive oil
- 4 tbsp. sour cream
- A little salt
- A little black pepper

INSTRUCTIONS

1. Dice the bacon, then add it to a bowl and combine with the rest of the ingredients. Stir well.
2. Take the muffin moulds and fill them 2/3 of the way to the top with the mixture.
3. Preheat your Air Fryer to 160°C/320°F.
4. SAdd the muffins to the basket and cook for 20 minutes, checking once. Serve and enjoy.

THE AIR FRYER COOKBOOK FOR BEGINNERS

6 | BREAKFAST IDEAS

1. Veggie egg muffins
2. Spanish omelette
3. Mediterranean omelette
4. Scrambled eggs with mushrooms
5. English breakfast
6. Balanced quesadilla
7. Keto avocado eggs
8. Baked oatmeal with strawberry jam
9. Stuffed apples with nuts and seeds
10. Vegan spinach burritos
11. Catalan croquets
12. Mixed canapes
13. Quinoa frittata
14. Seed and nut granola
15. Bread pizza with eggs
16. Crispy bacon and veggie sandwich
17. Homemade parmesan crackers
18. Egg bread with blue cheese and salad
19. Parmesan sausage frittata
20. French breakfast
21. Zucchini egg patties
22. Peanut-jelly toast
23. Broccoli casserole
24. Egg cups
25. Chocolate pudding with biscuits

DON'T FORGET TO
GET THE

TOP RECIPES FROM
THIS BOOK AS

**A DOWNLOADABLE
PDF IN COLOUR**

FOR FREE!

SCAN THE QR CODE BELOW

VEGGIE EGG MUFFINS

Egg muffins are a great option for healthy morning eating – and they can be pre-prepared!

Serving size: 2 portions

TOTAL CALORIES: 245
Fat: 13g | Carbs: 17g | Protein: 13g

INGREDIENTS

- 4 eggs
- 1 carrot
- 1 pepper
- 1 potato
- 1 tbsp. seed mix
- 1 tbsp. cottage cheese
- ½ tsp. salt
- A little parsley – optional

INSTRUCTIONS

1. Preheat your Air Fryer to 200°C/400°F.
2. Slice the veggies into small pieces and combine with the rest of the ingredients. Take the muffin moulds and fill them up to 2/3 of their total capacity.
3. Place the moulds in the basket and cook for 7-10 minutes.

SPANISH OMELETTE

A traditional, tasty and creamy omelette – perfect for your first meal of the day.

Serving size: 1 portion

TOTAL CALORIES: 420
Fat: 30g | Carbs: 20g | Protein: 16g

INGREDIENTS

- 1 medium potato
- 3 eggs
- 2 scallions
- 1 tbsp. olive oil
- Salt, to taste

INSTRUCTIONS

1. Preheat your Air Fryer to 200°C/400°F.
2. Finely dice the potatoes.
3. Add a little oil to the basket, then add the potatoes and cook for 5 minutes.
4. Dice the scallions and mix well with the eggs, olive oil, salt and cooked potatoes.
5. Take a circular pan that can fit into your Air Fryer and fill it with the omelette mixture. Add it to the Air Fryer and cook for 20 minutes.

MEDITERRANEAN OMELETTE

Mediterranean omelettes have no rules – simply add your favourite fresh Mediterranean veggies.

Serving size: 1 portion

TOTAL CALORIES: 264
Fat: 17g | Carbs: 11g | Protein: 12g

INGREDIENTS

- 2 eggs
- 1 green pepper
- 10 olives, pitted
- ½ tomato
- A little oil for the cooking basket
- A pinch of salt and pepper

INSTRUCTIONS

1. Preheat your Air Fryer to 200°C/400°F.
2. Cut the veggies into small pieces. Combine them with the eggs and spices.
3. Take a circular pan that can fit into your Air Fryer. Add a little oil and the egg mixture to it.
4. Place the pan in the basket and cook for 10 minutes.

SCRAMBLED EGGS WITH MUSHROOMS

Few children can say no to scrambled eggs – and this mushroom version is always a winner!

Serving size: 2 portions

TOTAL CALORIES: 398
Fat: 32g | Carbs: 2g | Protein: 22g

INGREDIENTS

- 3 white mushrooms
- 4 eggs
- Salt and pepper, to taste
- 1 tbsp. olive oil

INSTRUCTIONS

1. Preheat your Air Fryer to 200°C/400°F.
2. Cut the mushrooms into very thin slices. Combine them with the rest of the ingredients. Pour the mixture into a circular pan.
3. Place the pan in the basket and cook for 5 minutes. Open the basket and scramble the eggs a little. Close the basket and cook for a further 5 minutes.

ENGLISH BREAKFAST

A full, nutritious meal with a high energy value.

Serving size: 2 portions

TOTAL CALORIES: 563
Fat: 30g | Carbs: 43g | Protein: 25g

INGREDIENTS

- 2 thin sausages
- 4 slices bacon
- 2 eggs
- 4 tbsp. canned black beans
- 1 tomato
- 2 slices bread

INSTRUCTIONS

1. Preheat your Air Fryer to 200°C/400°F.
2. Open the basket and add two sausages, the bacon, and the eggs (cracked in silicone moulds). Cook for 10 minutes.
3. Remove the first batch from the Air Fryer and add the slices of tomato and pieces of bread. Cook for 10 minutes.
4. Serve both batches together and enjoy. One serving should contain: one egg, one sausage, two slices bacon, canned beans, sliced tomato and bread.

BALANCED QUESADILLA

A morning quesadilla is guaranteed to result in a good start to your day!

Serving size: 1 portion

TOTAL CALORIES: 250
Fat: 10g | Carbs: 24g | Protein: 9g

INGREDIENTS

- 1 tortilla
- ¼ cup grated cheddar cheese
- 1 tbsp. sriracha
- 1 tomato
- 1 small red pepper
- A little oil for the cooking basket

INSTRUCTIONS

1. Preheat your Air Fryer to 200°C/400°F.
2. Spread little sriracha over the tortilla and add the cheese. Cut the tomato and pepper. Add them to the tortilla.
3. Add a little oil to the basket, then add the tortilla and cook it (unfolded) for 5 minutes. Open the basket, fold the tortilla in half and cook for a further 5 minutes.

KETO AVOCADO EGGS

Every diet deserves a tasty start to the day – and this could be your new favourite keto breakfast.

Serving size: 1 portion

TOTAL CALORIES: 386
Fat: 35g | Carbs: 1g | Protein: 12g

INGREDIENTS

- 1 avocado
- 2 eggs
- 1 scallion
- Oregano, to taste
- Salt, to taste
- A little oil for the cooking basket

INSTRUCTIONS

1. Preheat your Air Fryer to 180°C/360°F.
2. Cut the avocado in half and remove the stone. Dice the scallion. Add one egg to every half avocado, then sprinkle it with scallions, oregano and salt.
3. Add a little oil to the basket, the add the two halves of avocado and cook for 15 minutes. Serve and enjoy.

BAKED OATMEAL WITH STRAWBERRY JAM

Oatmeal is a natural source of inulin – a type of fibre that helps maintain a healthy gut.

Serving size: 2 portions

TOTAL CALORIES: 410
Fat: 17g | Carbs: 50g | Protein: 10g

INGREDIENTS

- ½ cup rolled oats
- 1 tbsp. peanut butter
- 1 tsp. cocoa powder
- ½ cup blueberries
- 1 cup milk
- ½ cup water
- 1 tsp. honey

INSTRUCTIONS

1. Preheat your Air Fryer to 160°C/320°F.
2. Combine all ingredients. Take two oven-proof bowls and fill them with the mixture.
3. Place the bowls in the Air Fryer basket and cook for 7 minutes.

STUFFED APPLES WITH NUTS AND SEEDS

This Turkish-inspired breakfast meal will certainly be a treat for all your senses!

Serving size: 4 portions

TOTAL CALORIES: 334
Fat: 16g | Carbs: 42g | Protein: 3g

INGREDIENTS

- 4 apples
- ½ cup walnuts
- 2 tbsp. oat flakes
- 1 tbsp. honey
- 2 tbsp. orange juice

INSTRUCTIONS

1. Preheat your Air Fryer to 160°C/320°F.
2. Make a hole through the middle of every apple. Crush or blend the walnuts, then combine them with the oats, honey and orange juice. Fill each apple hole with the walnut mixture.
3. Add aluminium foil to the basket, then add the apples. Cook for 12-13 minutes, checking once

VEGAN SPINACH BURRITOS

A breakfast burrito is the champion of breakfasts, and this vegan version is definitely a winner.

Serving size: 2 portions

TOTAL CALORIES: 137
Fat: 14g | Carbs: 45g | Protein: 13g

INGREDIENTS

- 2 tortillas
- 2 tbsp. guacamole
- 2 tbsp. peanut butter
- 2 pcs. vegan cheese
- 1 cup cooked rice

INSTRUCTIONS

1. Preheat your Air Fryer to 200°C/400°F.
2. Spread guacamole and peanut butter over the tortillas, then add the rice and vegan cheese. Wrap them well.
3. Place the tortillas in the Air Fryer basket and cook for 6 minutes.

CATALAN CROQUETS

Easy to prepare, this is a Spanish-inspired tapas recipe.

Serving size: 4 portions

TOTAL CALORIES: 212
Fat: 11g | Carbs: 18g | Protein: 10g

INGREDIENTS

- 1 bag/400g/14oz frozen bechamel ham croquets
- Sour cream
- 1 cucumber
- A little oil for the cooking basket

INSTRUCTIONS

1. Preheat your Air Fryer to 200°C/400°F.
2. Add a little oil to the basket, then add the croquets and cook for 5 minutes on both sides.
3. Serve with sour cream and slices of cucumber.

MIXED CANAPES

A super easy preparation and a tasty result will make these capapes incredibly popular with your guests.

Serving size: 2 portions

TOTAL CALORIES: 302
Fat: 8g | Carbs: 36g | Protein: 21g

INGREDIENTS

- 10 slices baguette bread
- ¼ cup grated parmesan
- ¼ cup grated gouda
- 2 pieces smoked salmon
- 1 tomato
- A couple of olives
- Fresh basil, to taste

INSTRUCTIONS

1. Preheat your Air Fryer to 200°C/400°F.
2. On half of the bread pieces add gouda, then to the other half add parmesan.
3. Place the bread pieces in the basket and cook for 5 minutes.
4. Add slices of tomato and the olives to the gouda-covered bread. To the bread parmesan-covered bread, add smoked salmon and basil leaves.

QUINOA FRITTATA

This egg-based frittata has a creamy texture and is full to the brim with healthy vegetables.

Serving size: 3 portions

TOTAL CALORIES: 191
Fat: 15g | Carbs: 22g | Protein: 32g

INGREDIENTS

- 1 cup broccoli
- 2 cups chicken broth
- ½ cup quinoa
- ½ zucchini
- 5 eggs
- 1 tbsp. olive oil
- A pinch of salt
- Curry powder, to taste

INSTRUCTIONS

1. Add the chicken broth, quinoa, broccoli and zucchini to a pan over medium heat. Let simmer for 10 minutes.
2. Beat the eggs, then add the (drained) boiled ingredients, olive oil and spices.
3. Take a cooking pan that can fit in your Air Fryer basket. Add the egg mixture and cook for 15 minutes.

SEED AND NUT GRANOLA

Many store-bought granolas are a high source of sugar. Try this home-prepared version instead, which is not only fast and more economical, but also healthier.

Serving size: 3 portions

TOTAL CALORIES: 296
Fat: 15g | Carbs: 60g | Protein: 9g

INGREDIENTS

- ½ cup rolled oats
- ½ cup dried cranberries
- 2 tbsp. sunflower seeds
- 2 tbsp. chia seeds
- ¼ cup chopped almonds
- 2 tbsp. maple syrup

INSTRUCTIONS

1. Preheat your Air Fryer to 180°C/320°F.
2. Combine all ingredients in a bowl, taking care to ensure that the maple syrup is mixed in well.
3. Add the mixture to the basket and cook for 13 minutes. Store in a jar or serve it immediately.

BREAD PIZZA WITH EGGS

Excellent for using up old pieces of bread!

Serving size: 3 portions

TOTAL CALORIES: 316

Fat: 15g | Carbs: 23g | Protein: 18g

INGREDIENTS

- 4 slices bread
- 3 eggs
- 4 slices ham
- A pinch of oregano
- 100g/3.5oz mozzarella
- ¼ cup tomato sauce
- Salt, to taste
- A little oil for the cooking basket

INSTRUCTIONS

1. Preheat your Air Fryer to 200°C/400°F.
2. Beat the eggs then combine with grated bread pieces. Take a cooking pan that fits your Air Fryer basket and fill it with the egg mixture.
3. Cook for 5 minutes, then open the basket and arrange the pizza toppings. Spread with tomato sauce, then add mozzarella and slices of ham. Sprinkle with oregano. Bake for a further 7 minutes.

CRISPY BACON AND VEGGIE SANDWICH

This recipe is solid proof that the Air Fryer is the ultimate crisper – without oil!

Serving size: 2 portions

TOTAL CALORIES: 264

Fat: 7g | Carbs: 36g | Protein: 9g

INGREDIENTS

- 4 slices bread
- 4 slices bacon
- 1 green pepper
- ¼ zucchini
- 2 tbsp. hummus
- A little oil for the cooking basket

INSTRUCTIONS

1. Preheat your Air Fryer to 180°C/360°F.
2. Cut the pepper and zucchini into thin slices. Take two pieces of bread and spread hummus over them, then add bacon, zucchini and pepper. Sandwich the fillings with another slice of bread.
3. Place the two sandwiches in the Air Fryer basket and cook for 7 minutes.

HOMEMADE PARMESAN CRACKERS

These crackers are a gentle alternative for your stomach.

Serving size: 2 portions

(IN MINUTES)
PREP 10
COOK 7

TOTAL CALORIES: 290

Fat: 23g | Carbs: 8g | Protein: 13g

INGREDIENTS

- 4 graham crackers
- 2 tbsp. butter
- ½ cup grated parmesan
- 2 small sausages
- 2 fresh tomatoes

INSTRUCTIONS

1. Preheat your Air Fryer to 200°C/400°F.
2. Spread the butter over every cracker and add a little parmesan to each.
3. Place the crackers and sausages in the Air Fryer basket. Cook for 7 minutes.
4. Each serving contains two crackers, one sausage and a mini tomato salad.

EGG BREAD WITH BLUE CHEESE AND SALAD

Egg bread might sound like a unique breakfast food, but some cultures swear by it!

Serving size: 2 portions

(IN MINUTES)
PREP 5
COOK 10

TOTAL CALORIES: 332

Fat: 12g | Carbs: 37g | Protein: 16g

INGREDIENTS

- 3 eggs
- 4 slices bread
- A pinch of salt
- 4 slices blue cheese
- Green salad
- Olive oil
- Balsamic vinegar

INSTRUCTIONS

1. Beat the eggs with a little salt, then soak every piece of bread in the egg mixture.
2. Preheat your Air Fryer to 200°C/400°F.
3. Add the soaked bread to the basket and cook for 5 minutes. Then, open the basket and add blue cheese to every slice of bread. Cook for a further 5 minutes.
4. Serve with a green salad dressed in olive oil and balsamic vinegar.

THE AIR FRYER COOKBOOK FOR BEGINNERS

PARMESAN SAUSAGE FRITTATA

This easy recipe simply requires you to combine the ingredients and enjoy.

Serving size: 3 portions

TOTAL CALORIES: 174
Fat: 10g | Carbs: 6g | Protein: 14g

INGREDIENTS

- 4 eggs
- 1 grated carrot
- ½ cup grated parmesan
- 2 pork sausages
- A pinch of salt

INSTRUCTIONS

1. Preheat your Air Fryer to 200°C/400°F.
2. Cut the sausages into small pieces and place them in the basket. Cook for 5 minutes.
3. In a bowl, combine the eggs, parmesan, carrot and cooked sausage. Add a little salt, to taste.
4. Take a cooking pan that can fit in your Air Fryer basket. Place the egg mixture inside and cook for 15 minutes.

FRENCH BREAKFAST

A lovely start to the morning, this recipe is full of protein, carbs and joy.

Serving size: 2 portions

TOTAL CALORIES: 245
Fat: 10g | Carbs: 30g | Protein: 7g

INGREDIENTS

- 2 eggs
- 2 frozen croissants
- 2 tbsp. strawberry jam
- 2 cups orange juice

INSTRUCTIONS

1. Preheat your Air Fryer to 180°C/360°F.
2. Add the whole eggs to the Air Fryer basket, then add the croissants. Cook for 9 minutes.
3. Serve with glass of orange juice and strawberry jam.

ZUCCHINI EGG PATTIES

A quick and easy breakfast that can also be packed away for later.

Serving size: 4 portions

TOTAL CALORIES: 320
Fat: 17g | Carbs: 31g | Protein: 6g

INGREDIENTS

- 1 zucchini
- 2 eggs
- 1 tbsp. cottage cheese
- Salt, to taste
- 1 sheet puff pastry

INSTRUCTIONS

1. Grate the zucchini and combine it with the egg and cottage cheese. Add a little salt.
2. Cut the puff pastry into 4cm squares. Fill the centre of each square with the egg mixture then fold into triangles. Seal the edges with a fork.
3. Preheat your Air Fryer to 200°C/400°F.
4. Add the pastries to the basket and bake for 12 minutes, checking once or twice throughout.

PEANUT-JELLY TOAST

A classic combination, there's nothing better than peanut and jelly for breakfast.

Serving size: 2 portions

TOTAL CALORIES: 265
Fat: 9g | Carbs: 36g | Protein: 7g

INGREDIENTS

- 4 slices bread
- 2 tbsp. peanut butter
- 2 tbsp. strawberry jam
- A little oil for the cooking basket

INSTRUCTIONS

1. Preheat your Air Fryer to 200°C/400°F.
2. On the inner side of the bread spread peanut butter and strawberry jam. Place two pieces of bread together to form a sandwich.
3. Add a little oil to the basket, then place the two sandwiches in the basket and cook for 7 minutes.

BROCCOLI CASSEROLE

A delicious mix of broccoli and cheese couscous in the form of the perfect breakfast casserole.

Serving size: 3 portions

TOTAL CALORIES: 226

Fat: 11g | Carbs: 16g | Protein: 12g

INGREDIENTS

- 2 cups broccoli
- 1 cup milk
- 1 cup grated cheddar cheese
- 2 eggs
- 4 tbsp. couscous
- A pinch of salt

INSTRUCTIONS

1. Cut the broccoli into very small pieces. Combine all the ingredients in a cooking pan.
2. Preheat the Air Fryer to 160°C/320°F.
3. Place the cooking pan in the Air Fryer basket and cook for 18 minutes.

EGG CUPS

Some breakfasts spoil your senses (in a good way!) – and this is definitely one of them.

Serving size: 3 portions

TOTAL CALORIES: 197

Fat: 12g | Carbs: 6g | Protein: 12g

INGREDIENTS

- 6 eggs
- 3 peppers
- 1 tomato
- 2 slices bacon
- 3 tbsp. feta cheese

INSTRUCTIONS

1. Dice the peppers, tomato and bacon. Crumble the cheese with your hands.
2. Combine all ingredients in a bowl.
3. Fill the silicone muffin moulds halfway, then place them in the Air Fryer basket. Cook for 12 minutes at 180°C/360°F.

CHOCOLATE PUDDING WITH BISCUITS

This delightful homemade pudding is good enough to serve as a meal.

Serving size: 2 portions

TOTAL CALORIES: 289
Fat: 6g | Carbs: 47g | Protein: 10g

INGREDIENTS

- 4 tbsp. millet
- 2 tbsp. honey
- 1 tbsp. cocoa powder
- 1 ½ cup milk
- Vanilla stick

INSTRUCTIONS

1. Combine all ingredients in a bowl.
2. Fill four silicone muffin moulds with the mixture.
3. Preheat the Air Fryer to 180°C/360°F. Add the cups to the basket and bake for 12 minutes.

7 | WRAPS & SANDWICHES

1. Sicilian pepperoni wrap
2. Mozzarella wrap
3. Pesto and tomato wrap
4. Chicken avocado wrap
5. Vegan hummus wrap
6. Keto beef wrap
7. Juicy egg wrap
8. Gordon Ramsey sriracha sandwich
9. Grilled cheese sandwich
10. Sweet mustard and ham sandwich
11. Avocado and bacon sandwich
12. Tzatziki sandwich with chicken
13. Tuna sandwich

DON'T FORGET TO GET THE

TOP RECIPES FROM THIS BOOK AS

A DOWNLOADABLE PDF IN COLOUR

FOR FREE!

SCAN THE QR CODE BELOW

SICILIAN PEPPERONI WRAP

(IN MINUTES)
PREP
5
COOK
6

Make this wrap ahead of time and enjoy it when the time is right.

Serving size: 2 portions

TOTAL CALORIES: 271
Fat: 11g | Carbs: 30g | Protein: 9g

INGREDIENTS

- 2 tortillas
- 2 slices cheddar cheese
- 2 pcs. mozzarella
- 6 pcs. pepperoni
- 2 pickles
- 2 tbsp. tomato sauce

INSTRUCTIONS

1. Preheat your Air Fryer to 200°C/400°F.
2. Add the cheese, mozzarella, pepperoni, sliced pickles, and tomato sauce to the tortillas. Wrap like a burrito.
3. Place the two tortillas in the Air Fryer basket and cook for 6 minutes.

MOZZARELLA WRAP

(IN MINUTES)
PREP
15
COOK
6

Mozzarella is a mild yet tasty addition to any sandwich or wrap.

Serving size: 2 portions

TOTAL CALORIES: 265
Fat: 11g | Carbs: 23g | Protein: 22g

INGREDIENTS

- 200g/7oz mozzarella
- 2 tortillas
- A handful of basil
- 1 tomato
- Salt, to taste

INSTRUCTIONS

1. Preheat your Air Fryer to 200°C/400°F.
2. Cut the mozzarella and tomato into thin slices. Place the mozzarella, tomato, and basil on the tortillas, then sprinkle with salt. Wrap like a burrito.
3. Place the two tortillas in the basket and cook for 6 minutes.

THE AIR FRYER COOKBOOK FOR BEGINNERS

PESTO AND TOMATO WRAP

3

Some recipes are pure gold – and this pesto sauce may be green, but it can be added to a huge variety of dishes, including this delicious wrap.

Serving size: 2 portions

TOTAL CALORIES: 275
Fat: 14g | Carbs: 25g | Protein: 10g

INGREDIENTS

- 2 tortillas
- 2 tbsp. pesto sauce
- 1 green pepper
- ½ cup grated yellow cheese
- 2 mushrooms

INSTRUCTIONS

1. Preheat your Air Fryer to 200°C/400°F.
2. Dice the pepper and mushrooms. Spread pesto sauce over the tortilla and add the cheese, mushrooms and pepper. Wrap like a burrito.
3. Place the two tortillas in the Air Fryer basket and cook for 6 minutes.

CHICKEN AVOCADO WRAP

4

This easy to prepare and quick to pack meal is the perfect lunch on the go.

Serving size: 2 portions

TOTAL CALORIES: 325
Fat: 13g | Carbs: 23g | Protein: 25g

INGREDIENTS

- 2 tortillas
- 2 pcs. white chicken
- ½ avocado
- 2 tbsp. hummus
- 2 tbsp. parmesan
- A pinch of salt

INSTRUCTIONS

1. Preheat your Air Fryer to 200°C/400°F.
2. Add a little oil to the basket, then place the two chicken pieces in the basket, add little salt and cook for 10 minutes.
3. On ¼ of the tortilla add a little avocado, on the following ¼ add humus, on the next ¼ add parmesan and on the last ¼ add cooked chicken. Fold the tortilla into a triangle.
4. Place the two tortillas in the basket and cook for 6 minutes.

VEGAN HUMMUS WRAP

This vegan alternative is high in protein, tasty, juicy and easy to prepare.

Serving size: 2 portions

TOTAL CALORIES: 247
Fat: 11g | Carbs: 27g | Protein: 9g

INGREDIENTS

- 2 tortillas
- 2 tbsp. hummus
- 10 boneless olives
- 2 tbsp. pumpkin seeds
- 1 tomato
- 2 tbsp. canned peas
- A pinch of salt

INSTRUCTIONS

1. Preheat your Air Fryer to 200°C/400°F.
2. Spread the hummus over the tortillas, then add olives, peas, seeds and chopped tomato. Sprinkle with a little salt and wrap like a burrito.
3. Place the two tortillas in the basket and cook for 6 minutes.

KETO BEEF WRAP

Rice leaves can be found in most markets and are low in calories and carbohydrates.

Serving size: 2 portions

TOTAL CALORIES: 352
Fat: 22g | Carbs: 8g | Protein: 31g

INGREDIENTS

- 200g/7oz beef
- A little oil for the cooking basket
- A pinch of salt
- 4 rice leaves
- 1 carrot
- 1 cup grated cabbage
- Carb-free Caesar sauce

INSTRUCTIONS

1. Preheat your Air Fryer to 200°C/400°F.
2. Cut the beef into thin slices.
3. Add a little oil to the basket, then add the beef and bake for 10 minutes.
4. Add the chopped carrots, cabbage, cooked beef and Caesar sauce to the rice leaves. Wrap like a burrito.
5. Place the wraps in the basket and cook for 6 minutes.

JUICY EGG WRAP

There's no end to what you can put in an Air Fryer wrap!

Serving size: 2 portions

TOTAL CALORIES: 285

Fat: 15g | Carbs: 23g | Protein: 12g

INGREDIENTS

- 2 scrambled eggs (see the recipe for scrambled eggs)
- 2 tortillas
- ½ cup grated blue cheese
- 2 tbsp. sriracha

INSTRUCTIONS

1. Preheat your Air Fryer to 200°C/400°F.
2. Add the scrambled eggs, blue cheese and sriracha sauce to the tortillas. Wrap them like a burrito.
3. Place the two tortillas in the basket and cook for 6 minutes.

GORDON RAMSEY SRIRACHA SANDWICH

Made with two types of cheese, this sandwich will be love at first sight.

Serving size: 2 portions

TOTAL CALORIES: 412

Fat: 25g | Carbs: 33g | Protein: 13g

INGREDIENTS

- 4 slices bread
- 2 pcs. Romano cheese
- 2 pcs. asiago cheese
- 2 tbsp. sriracha
- 2 tbsp. butter

INSTRUCTIONS

1. Preheat your Air Fryer to 200°C/400°F.
2. Spread butter on the outer side of each slice of bread. On the inside, spread sriracha and add one piece of Romano and one piece of asiago cheese. Form a sandwich with two pieces of bread.
3. Add the two sandwiches to the basket and cook for 6 minutes.

GRILLED CHEESE SANDWICH

A classic for a reason.

Serving size: 2 portions

TOTAL CALORIES: 500
Fat: 32g | Carbs: 34g | Protein: 14g

INGREDIENTS

- 4 slices bread
- 2 pcs. gouda cheese
- 2 pcs. Havarti cheese
- 2 pcs. cheddar cheese
- 2 tbsp. butter

INSTRUCTIONS

1. Preheat your Air Fryer to 200°C/400°F.
2. Spread butter on the outer side of each slice of bread. On the inner side, add the three types of cheese. Form a sandwich with two pieces of bread.
3. Add the two sandwiches to the basket and cook for 6 minutes.

SWEET MUSTARD AND HAM SANDWICH

Ham paired with sweet mustard sauce is a combination guaranteed to bring a smile to your face.

Serving size: 2 portions

TOTAL CALORIES: 457
Fat: 27g | Carbs: 42g | Protein: 11g

INGREDIENTS

- 4 slices bread
- 4 pcs. ham
- 1 tbsp. olive oil
- 1 tbsp. honey
- 2 tbsp. mustard
- A pinch of salt
- 2 slices yellow cheese
- 2 tbsp. butter

INSTRUCTIONS

1. Preheat your Air Fryer to 200°C/400°F.
2. In a small bowl, combine the honey, mustard, olive oil and salt.
3. Spread butter on the outer side of each slice of bread. On the inside of each slice, spread the mustard mixture, then add ham and cheese. Form a sandwich with two pieces of bread.
4. Add the two sandwiches to the basket and cook for 6 minutes.

THE AIR FRYER COOKBOOK FOR BEGINNERS

AVOCADO AND BACON SANDWICH

If you're someone who can't get enough of sandwiches, you're in luck – this is a clear winner in the sandwich stakes!

Serving size: 2 portions

TOTAL CALORIES: 398
Fat: 24g | Carbs:34g | Protein: 8g

INGREDIENTS

- 4 slices bread
- ½ avocado
- 4 slices bacon
- 2 tbsp. butter

INSTRUCTIONS

1. Preheat your Air Fryer to 200°C/400°F.
2. Spread butter on the outer side of each slice of bread. On the inside of each slice, add slices of avocado and bacon. Form a sandwich with two pieces of bread.
3. Add the two sandwiches to the basket and cook for 6 minutes.

TZATZIKI SANDWICH WITH CHICKEN

An inspiring Mediterranean combination.

Serving size: 2 portions

TOTAL CALORIES: 430
Fat: 20g | Carbs: 36g | Protein: 23g

INGREDIENTS

- 4 slices bread
- 1 pc. Fresh white chicken filet
- 2 tbsp. tzatziki sauce
- ½ cup grated cheddar cheese
- 2 tbsp. butter

INSTRUCTIONS

1. Preheat your Air Fryer to 200°C/400°F.
2. Add a little oil to the basket, then add the chicken filet and cook for 10 minutes.
3. Shred the cooked chicken and combine it with the tzatziki sauce. Spread butter on the outer side of each slice of bread. On the inside of each bread slice, add the chicken-tzatziki and cheddar cheese. Form a sandwich with two pieces of bread.
4. Add the two sandwiches to the basket and cook for 6 minutes.

TUNA SANDWICH

A classic summer sandwich.

Serving size: 2 portions

(IN MINUTES)
PREP
10
COOK
6

TOTAL CALORIES: 278
Fat: 6g | Carbs: 35g | Protein: 19g

INGREDIENTS

- 4 slices bread
- 100g/3.5oz tuna
- 1 tomato
- 2 pickles
- A little oil for the cooking basket

INSTRUCTIONS

1. Preheat your Air Fryer to 200°C/400°F.
2. Add the tuna, chopped tomatoes and pickles to the slices of bread. Form a sandwich with two pieces of bread.
3. Add a little oil to the basket, then add the two sandwiches and cook for 6 minutes.

THANK YOU FOR BUYING THIS COOKBOOK BY
FEARNE PRENTICE!

DON'T FORGET TO GET THE
TOP 100 RECIPES FROM THIS BOOK AS

A PDF IN COLOUR

FOR FREE!

SCAN THE QR CODE ABOVE AND GET ACCESS TO THE FREE PDF IN COLOUR.

PLEASE NOTE THAT THE PDF IS NOT FOR SALE OR DISTRIBUTION AND IS ONLY INTENDED FOR PERSONAL USE. A BREACH OF THIS CONDITION IS CONSIDERED COPYRIGHT INFRINGEMENT

8 | MAIN DISHES WITH BEEF

1. Korean soy beef with rice
2. Onion beef stew
3. Beef burgers with salsa
4. Meatball pasta
5. Peanut butter beef
6. Rolled ground beef and egg
7. Mexican beef salad
8. Beef soup with cheese toast
9. Creamy mushroom and beef stew
10. Beef zucchini skewers
11. Meatballs in a tomato-basil sauce
12. Beefsteak with small potatoes
13. Strawberry steak salad
14. Sweet-and-sour tacos with beef
15. Roasted beef with cherry tomatoes and peppers
16. Baked beef hot dog
17. Mini beef pies
18. Keto Italian beef salad
19. Beef pita bread
20. Stewed beef with mushrooms
21. Pasta Bolognese
22. Pumpkin stew with meatballs
23. Fried beef with sesame and beans
24. Marinated beef for quesadillas
25. Beef strips with curry
26. Beef risotto
27. Bacon-wrapped beef strips and spinach
28. Beef and veggie nachos
29. Beef-stuffed eggplants
30. Ground beef puffed bombs
31. Traditional mashed potatoes and meatloaf
32. Rolled beef with mozzarella
33. Mini taquitos with sriracha

DON'T FORGET TO GET THE

TOP RECIPES FROM THIS BOOK AS

A DOWNLOADABLE PDF IN COLOUR

FOR FREE!

SCAN THE QR CODE BELOW

KOREAN SOY BEEF WITH RICE

This lunch meal will give you the energy you need to reach the end of your day in high spirits.

Serving size: 2 portions

TOTAL CALORIES: 435

Fat: 23g | Carbs: 27g | Protein: 25g

INGREDIENTS

- 200g/7oz beef
- 3 tbsp. soy sauce
- 1 clove of garlic
- 1 tbsp. sugar
- ½ tbsp. salt
- 1 cup rice
- 2 cups vegetable broth
- 2 tbsp. olive oil

INSTRUCTIONS

1. Cut the beef into thin slices. Chop the garlic. Combine the meat with the soy sauce, garlic, sugar and salt. Marinade it for 15 minutes.
2. While the meat is marinading, prepare the rice. Take a cooking pan that can fit in your Air Fryer basket and combine the rice, vegetable broth, a little salt and the olive oil. Cook it for 12 minutes at 120°C/240°F.
3. Take the rice out of the basket and add the meat. Cook for 20 minutes at 180°C/360°F.

ONION BEEF STEW

A classic stew prepared quicker than you could have ever imagined.

Serving size: 2 portions

TOTAL CALORIES: 510

Fat: 24g | Carbs: 43g | Protein: 26g

INGREDIENTS

- 200g/7oz beef
- 2 white onions
- 1 cup vegetable broth
- 2 tbsp. Worcestershire sauce
- 2 cups small potatoes
- 2 tbsp. butter
- Salt, to taste
- Pepper, to taste

INSTRUCTIONS

1. Dice the onions. Cut the meat into two pieces and add it to a cooking pan that fits in your Air Fryer. Add the onions, Worcestershire sauce, a little salt and the broth.
2. Cook for 20 minutes at 180°C/360°F.
3. Toss the potatoes with the salt and butter. Once the meat is ready, add the potatoes to the basket and bake for a further 15 minutes at the same temperature.
4. Serve with the sauce from the beef stew.

3 BEEF BURGERS WITH SALSA

Can anyone say no to a nice, juicy burger? You don't need to, with this healthy salad-supported version!

Serving size: 3 portions

TOTAL CALORIES: 430

Fat: 20g | Carbs: 27g | Protein: 32g

INGREDIENTS

- 300g/10.5oz ground beef
- 2 tbsp. breadcrumbs
- 1 egg
- 1 tsp. salt
- ½ tsp. chilli powder
- 3 burger buns
- 3 leaves of lettuce
- 1 tomato
- 3 tbsp. salsa – chilli optional
- A little oil for the cooking basket

INSTRUCTIONS

1. Combine the beef, egg, breadcrumbs, salt, and chilli powder in a bowl. Knead the meat until it is homogenized. With your hands, form three burger patties.
2. Add a little oil to the basket, then add the burger patties and cook at 160°C/320°F for 15 minutes, flipping them once.
3. Slice the burger buns through the middle and spread with salsa, then add the burger patty, lettuce leaves, and slices of tomato.

MEATBALL PASTA

This easy to make pasta dish will be popular in every household.

Serving size: 2 portions

TOTAL CALORIES: 132

Fat: 16g | Carbs: 42g | Protein: 30g

INGREDIENTS

- 200g/7oz ground beef
- ½ white onion
- ½ tsp. salt
- 1 tbsp. olive oil
- A pinch of black pepper
- 2 cups of cooked spaghetti
- ½ cup tomato sauce
- ½ tsp. garlic powder

INSTRUCTIONS

1. Finely dice the onion. Combine it with the meat, salt and oil. Use your hands to form small meatballs, you should get a total of 8.
2. Add a little oil to the basket, then add the meatballs and cook at 160°C/320°F for 15 minutes. Open the basket once to turn the meatballs.
3. Take a pan that can fit in the Air Fryer basket and add the cooked spaghetti, tomato sauce, garlic and meatballs. Mix a little, then cook for 5 minutes.

PEANUT BUTTER BEEF

This Asian-inspired dish sees peanut butter lend a soft touch to meaty beef.

Serving size: 2 portions

TOTAL CALORIES: 327

Fat: 20g | Carbs: 9g | Protein: 24g

INGREDIENTS

- 200g/7oz beef
- 2 carrots
- 1 onion
- 1 garlic clove
- 1 tsp. smoked paprika
- ½ tsp. black pepper
- 1 tbsp. peanut butter
- 1 handful crushed peanuts
- ½ cup vegetable broth
- 1 tsp. curry powder
- ½ tsp. salt
- 1 tbsp. olive oil

INSTRUCTIONS

1. Slice the carrot and dice the garlic and onion, then cut the beef into thin slices.
2. Take a cooking pan and combine all ingredients, mixing them well so the peanut butter is dissolved.
3. Place the cooking pan in the Air Fryer basket and cook for 20 minutes at 140°C/280°F.

ROLLED GROUND BEEF AND EGG

This dish might take a little more preparation than most, but it tastes like heaven!

Serving size: 3 portions

TOTAL CALORIES: 276

Fat: 18.3g | Carbs: 4g | Protein: 22g

INGREDIENTS

- 200g/7oz ground beef
- 1 tbsp. breadcrumbs
- 1 egg
- ½ tsp. salt
- 2 boiled eggs
- 1 lettuce
- 10 cherry tomatoes
- 10 olives
- 2 tbsp. olive oil
- 1 tbsp. balsamic vinegar

INSTRUCTIONS

1. Combine the meat, salt, egg (non-boiled), and breadcrumbs, and mix well. On a flat surface, set out plastic wrap and spread the meat across it in a 2cm layer. Add the two boiled and peeled eggs then roll the meat with the help of the plastic wrap. When done, it should look like a smooth circular roll.
2. Preheat your Air Fryer to 160°C/320°F.
3. Add a little oil to the basket, then add the meat roll and cook for 15 minutes. Open the basket once and flip the roll over.
4. Remove the meat roll, let it cool a little and then cut it into thick slices.
5. Serve with a nice salad containing lettuce, tomato, olives, and olive oil-balsamic dressing.

7 — MEXICAN BEEF SALAD

The perfect low-carb meal for healthy Air Fryer lovers.

Serving size: 2 portions

TOTAL CALORIES: 245
Fat: 17g | Carbs: 6g | Protein: 15g

INGREDIENTS

- 100g/3.5oz beef
- A handful of rocket
- 1 cucumber
- A handful of parsley
- 2 tbsp. canned chickpeas
- 5 cherry tomatoes
- 2 tbsp. olive oil
- 1 tbsp. apple vinegar
- Salt, to taste

INSTRUCTIONS

1. Preheat your Air Fryer to 200°C/400°F.
2. Cut the beef into very thin slices.
3. Add a little oil to the basket, then place the beef slices in the basket and cook for 10 minutes. Open once and flip the slices.
4. Prepare the salad. With a cucumber peeler, form cucumber slices and add them to a bowl. Then, add the rest of the ingredients – the beef slices can be added to the top. Dress the salad with olive oil and vinegar, then sprinkle with salt and enjoy.

8 — BEEF SOUP WITH CHEESE TOAST

You'll love this combination of warm soup high in protein and crispy, cheesy bread.

Serving size: 3 portions

TOTAL CALORIES: 267
Fat: 7g | Carbs: 31g | Protein: 19g

INGREDIENTS

- 150g/5.3oz beefsteak
- ½ cup quinoa
- 1 celery stick
- 1 carrot
- 2 cloves garlic
- 1 ½ cup beef stock
- ½ tsp. salt
- 1 tsp. flour
- 1 tbsp. tomato sauce
- 3 slices bread
- ½ cup grated cheddar cheese

INSTRUCTIONS

1. Cut the beefsteak into small cubes. Grate the celery stick and carrot. Take a cooking pan that fits in the Air Fryer basket and add the chopped meat, quinoa, celery, carrot, garlic cloves, beef stock, salt and flour.
2. Preheat the Air Fryer to 130°C/260°F and place the pan in the basket. Cook for 20 minutes.
3. In the meantime, spread cheese over the bread. Once the soup is ready, add the pieces of bread to the Air Fryer basket and cook for 5 minutes.
4. Serve a bowl of the soup with a slice of the cheese bread.

CREAMY MUSH-ROOM AND BEEF STEW

A classic mushroom dish with added soft beefsteak.

Serving size: 2 portions

TOTAL CALORIES: 222
Fat: 12g | Carbs: 2g | Protein: 26g

INGREDIENTS

- 200g/7oz beefsteak
- 60g/2.1oz dried porcini mushrooms
- 80ml heavy cream
- ½ tsp. salt
- ½ tsp. black pepper
- A handful of parmesan

INSTRUCTIONS

1. Preheat your Air Fryer to 200°C/400°F.
2. Cut the beefsteak into two pieces and sprinkle with a little salt.
3. Add a little oil to the Air Fryer basket, then add the steak and cook for 10 minutes.
4. In a food processor, combine the mushrooms, heavy cream, salt and pepper. Blend until smooth.
5. Take a cooking pan and add the beefsteak and mushroom sauce. Place the pan in the basket and cook for 10 minutes at 140°C/280°F. Open the basket and sprinkle with parmesan. Cook for one more minute. Serve and enjoy.

BEEF ZUCCHINI SKEWERS

A must-have recipe for Sunday gatherings with friends, this dish doesn't require a grill or a big backyard.

Serving size: 3 portions

TOTAL CALORIES: 235
Fat: 14g | Carbs: 2g | Protein: 24g

INGREDIENTS

- 300g/10.5oz beefsteak
- 1 zucchini
- 2 tbsp. mustard
- 1 tsp. salt
- 1 tsp. paprika pepper
- 1 tbsp. olive oil

INSTRUCTIONS

1. Cut the zucchini and beefsteak into 2cm cubes. Place them in a bowl and toss with mustard, oil, salt and paprika. Take the skewer sticks and add one cube of meat then one cube of zucchini, until the skewer is full.
2. Preheat your Air Fryer to 170°C/340°F.
3. Add a little oil to the basket, then add the skewers to the basket and cook for 12 minutes, flipping once.

MEATBALLS IN A TOMATO-BASIL SAUCE

These meatballs can be served with any side dish, including rice, pasta or potatoes. The choice is yours!

Serving size: 3 portions

TOTAL CALORIES: 243
Fat: 12g | Carbs: 7g | Protein: 25g

iNGREDiENTS

- 300g/10.5oz ground beef
- 1 grated onion
- 1 tbsp. flour
- ½ tsp. salt
- A pinch of pepper
- 1 cup tomato sauce
- A handful of basil
- ½ tsp. oregano
- ½ tsp. garlic powder
- 1 tbsp. olive oil

iNSTRUCTIONS

1. Combine the ground meat, grated onion, flour, salt and pepper, and mix well. Form 10-12 meatballs.
2. Preheat your Air Fryer to 160°C/320°F.
3. Add a little oil to the basket, then place the meatballs in the basket and cook for 15 minutes, shaking once or twice.
4. Take a cooking pan, then add the tomato sauce, basil, garlic powder, oregano and oil. Add the cooked meatballs and place the pan in the Air Fryer basket. Cook for 5 minutes.

BEEFSTEAK WITH SMALL POTATOES

This beefsteak can be served rare, medium or well-done, with a variety of side dishes.

Serving size: 2 portions

TOTAL CALORIES: 66
Fat: 2.7g | Carbs: 8.1g | Protein: 4.9g

iNGREDiENTS

- 2 pieces of beefsteak
- 1 tbsp. mustard
- A little salt
- 1 tbsp. melted butter
- 2 cups small sweet potatoes
- A pinch of curry powder

iNSTRUCTIONS

1. Preheat your Air Fryer to 200°C/400°F.
2. Add a little oil to the basket. Spread mustard over the steaks then sprinkle with salt. Place them in the basket and cook for 15 minutes, flipping once.
3. Combined the unpeeled potatoes with the melted butter, salt and curry. Cook in the Air Fryer basket for 20 minutes, shaking once or twice.

⑬ STRAWBERRY STEAK SALAD

Strawberries have traditionally heralded the beginning of summer – and this is a salad for those who like to mix bold flavours and textures.

Serving size: 2 portions

TOTAL CALORIES: 502
Fat: 17g | Carbs: 20g | Protein: 37g

INGREDIENTS

- 100g/3.5oz beefsteak
- 1 tbsp. sriracha
- 1 cup strawberries
- ½ cup roasted salted almonds
- 2 tbsp. canned corn
- A handful of baby spinach
- 2 tbsp. olive oil
- A pinch of salt
- 1 tsp. apple vinegar

INSTRUCTIONS

1. Cut the steak into cubes and marinade it in the sriracha and a little salt.
2. Preheat your Air Fryer to 200°C/400°F.
3. Add a little oil to the basket, then add the steak and cook for 10 minutes.
4. Cut the strawberries in half, then shop the almonds into smaller pieces. Combine the meat with all the ingredients, then dress the salad with an oil-vinegar dressing. Sprinkle it with salt and enjoy.

⑭ SWEET-AND-SOUR TACOS WITH BEEF

There are thousands of different taco recipes, but beef tacos are a classic for a reason.

Serving size: 3 portions

TOTAL CALORIES: 246
Fat: 6g | Carbs: 27g | Protein: 21g

INGREDIENTS

- 3 tortillas
- 200g/7oz beefsteak
- ½ cup corn
- 1 cucumber
- 1 tbsp. honey
- 2 tomatoes
- 1 lime
- A little cilantro
- Salt, to taste

INSTRUCTIONS

1. Spread honey and a little salt over the beefsteak.
2. Preheat your Air Fryer to 120°C/240°F.
3. Add a little oil to the basket, then add the beefsteak and cook for 15 minutes, flipping once. Remove it from the Air Fryer and cut it into small pieces. Place the chopped beef back in the basket and cook at 200°C/400°F for a further 5 minutes.
4. Prepare the tortillas. Spread with a little beef, corn, chopped cucumber, chopped tomato and cilantro. Season with lime and salt, then serve and enjoy.

ROASTED BEEF WITH CHERRY TOMATOES AND PEPPERS

(IN MINUTES)
PREP 5
COOK 20

This light dish is easy on the stomach and full of fibre to aid in digestion.

Serving size: 2 portions

TOTAL CALORIES: 287

Fat: 15g | Carbs: 9g | Protein: 26g

INGREDIENTS

- 2 pcs. beefsteak
- ½ tsp. smoked paprika
- ½ tsp. salt
- 1 cup cherry tomatoes
- 2 green peppers
- 1 onion
- 1 tbsp. olive oil

INSTRUCTIONS

1. Preheat your Air Fryer to 200°C/400°F.
2. Slice the onion into small half-moons and combine with the beefsteak, paprika, salt and olive oil.
3. Add a little oil to the basket, then add the steak and onion mixture and cook for up to 13 minutes, flipping the steak once. Lower the temperature to 140°C/280°F, open the basket and add the tomatoes and peppers. Cook for a further 5 minutes.

BAKED BEEF HOT DOG

(IN MINUTES)
PREP 10
COOK 10

Hot dogs are guaranteed to inspire memories of being surrounded by people we love, and this recipe is no exception!

Serving size: 2 portions

TOTAL CALORIES: 286

Fat: 8g | Carbs: 32g | Protein: 22g

INGREDIENTS

- 150g/5.2oz beefsteak
- 2 tbsp. BBQ sauce
- A little salt
- 2 tbsp. mustard
- 2 hot dog buns
- 4 pickles
- ½ onion
- A little oil for the cooking basket

INSTRUCTIONS

1. Preheat your Air Fryer to 200°C/400°F.
2. Cut the beef into very thin slices. Toss with the BBQ sauce and salt.
3. Add a little oil to the basket, then add the beef and cook for 10 minutes.
4. Slice the hot dog bread though the centre and add a little mustard, beef, chopped pickles, and onion.

THE AIR FRYER COOKBOOK FOR BEGINNERS

MINI BEEF PIES

You can never have enough pie – so don't think twice about this recipe, and enjoy!

Serving size: 3 portions

TOTAL CALORIES: 564
Fat: 32g | Carbs: 51g | Protein: 15g

INGREDIENTS

- 100g/3.5oz beef
- 1 carrot
- 1 cup white mushrooms
- 2 scallions
- 1 cup broccoli
- 1 cup beef stock
- ½ cup heavy cream
- 1 sheet puff pastry
- 3 tbsp. salsa
- Salt, to taste

INSTRUCTIONS

1. Chop the vegetables into small pieces, followed by the beef.
2. Add the veggies, meat, beef stock, heavy cream and salt to a cooking pan that fits your Air Fryer. Combine well.
3. Preheat the Air Fryer to 170°C/340°F. Add the pan to the basket and cook for 10 minutes.
4. Meanwhile, take silicone muffin moulds and line them with puff pastry. Then, fill the cups with the meat mixture (a total of 6 cups) and top them with puff pastry.
5. Place the moulds in the Air Fryer basket and cook for 10 minutes at 180°C/360°F.

KETO ITALIAN BEEF SALAD

This dish combines crispy beef and salad for a low-carb meal that can be eaten with pleasure.

Serving size: 2 portions

TOTAL CALORIES: 356
Fat: 24g | Carbs: 3g | Protein: 26g

INGREDIENTS

- 150g/5.2oz beefsteak
- 1 cup cauliflower
- A handful of lettuce
- 2 boiled eggs
- 2 tbsp. sugar-free BBQ sauce
- 2 tbsp. olive oil
- Salt, to taste

INSTRUCTIONS

1. Preheat your Air Fryer to 160°C/320°F.
2. Sprinkle a little salt over the beefsteak.
3. Add a little oil to the basket, then place the beef and cauliflower in the basket and cook for 12 minutes, flipping the meat once.
4. When the meat is cooked, cut it into thin slices and let it chill.
5. Make a salad using the lettuce, egg slices, cauliflower, and BBQ sauce and olive oil dressing.

BEEF PITA BREAD

This Turkish-inspired recipe can be found on every corner of the city centre in Istanbul.

Serving size: 2 portions

TOTAL CALORIES: 280
Fat: 8g | Carbs: 25g | Protein: 28g

INGREDIENTS

- 200g/7oz ground beef
- 1 tbsp. chilli paprika
- ½ tsp. salt
- 1 clove garlic
- ½ onion
- 1 tbsp. breadcrumbs
- 2 pita breads
- 1 green pepper
- 1 tomato
- A handful of parsley

INSTRUCTIONS

1. Preheat your Air Fryer to 180°C/360°F.
2. Combine the meat, chilli paprika, breadcrumbs, salt, and blended garlic. Mix well.
3. Add the meat to a cooking pan and place the pan in the Air Fryer basket. Cook for 10 minutes, opening once to stir the mixture.
4. Slice the onion into half-moon shapes and chop the green pepper and tomato.
5. Add the meat, tomatoes, peppers, onion and parsley to the pita breads. Fold in half and serve.

STEWED BEEF WITH MUSHROOMS

Enjoy a variation of a classic – Air Fried. Delicious beef with perfectly cooked mushrooms! Ideal for a winters evening.

Serving size: 3 portions

TOTAL CALORIES: 334
Fat: 17g | Carbs: 13g | Protein: 26g

INGREDIENTS

- 300g/10.5oz beefsteak
- 2 cups white mushrooms
- 1 cup green peas
- 1 cup vegetable stock
- 1 onion
- 2 tbsp. olive oil
- ½ tbsp. salt
- ½ cup white wine

INSTRUCTIONS

1. Thinly slice the mushrooms and onion.
2. Place all the ingredients in a cooking pan that fits your Air Fryer.
3. Preheat the Air Fryer to 160°C/320°F. Place the cooking pan in the basket and cook for 20 minutes, flipping the steak once.
4. Before serving, cut the beef into three equal pieces.

PASTA BOLOGNESE

A true Italian classic that is super easy to prepare. It can be served with various types of pasta, including fusilli, spaghetti and penne.

Serving size: 3 portions

TOTAL CALORIES: 338
Fat: 6g | Carbs: 43g | Protein: 28g

INGREDIENTS

- 200g/7oz ground beef
- 2 cloves garlic
- 1 onion
- 1 cup tomato pasta
- 1 tsp. dried basil
- 3 cups cooked spaghetti

INSTRUCTIONS

1. Preheat your Air Fryer to 200°C/400°F.
2. Place the beef in a cooking pan in the Air Fryer and cook for 5 minutes.
3. Combine the tomato sauce, garlic, onion, salt and basil.
4. Open the basket and add the sauce to the meat. Mix well and cook for a further 5 minutes.
5. In a large bowl, combine the beef sauce with cooked spaghetti.

PUMPKIN STEW WITH MEATBALLS

Beef is popular all over the world – and this is a tasty Indian-inspired addition.

Serving size: 3 portions

TOTAL CALORIES: 357
Fat: 5g | Carbs: 52g | Protein: 26g

INGREDIENTS

- 300g/10.5oz ground beef
- 1 carrot
- 1 large sweet potato
- 1 cup pumpkin puree
- 1 tsp. salt
- A little rosemary
- 3 cups cooked rice

INSTRUCTIONS

1. Form 10-12 meatballs from the beef. Cut the carrots and potatoes into cubes.
2. In a cooking pan that fits your Air Fryer, combine the potatoes, carrots, beef, a little salt and rosemary.
3. Preheat the Air Fryer to 160°C/320°F and place the cooking pan in the basket. Cook for 15 minutes, stirring twice.
4. Serve with rice.

23 FRIED BEEF WITH SESAME AND BEANS

Serve this dish with cheese bread or olive crackers and it's perfect for a chilly day.

Serving size: 2 portions

TOTAL CALORIES: 422
Fat: 16g | Carbs: 30g | Protein: 38g

INGREDIENTS

- 200g/7oz beefsteak
- 2 tbsp. soy sauce
- 1 tbsp. honey
- ½ tsp. black pepper
- 1 tbsp. grated ginger
- 2 tbsp. sesame seeds
- ½ tsp. salt
- 2 cups canned green peas

INSTRUCTIONS

1. Cut the beef into thin, 4cm long pieces. Combine with the honey, soy sauce, black pepper, ginger, sesame seeds and salt.
2. Add the marinated meat to a cooking pan and then the Air Fryer basket. Cook at 180°C/360°F for 12 minutes.
3. Serve the crispy beef with green peas.

24 MARINATED BEEF FOR QUESADILLAS

How many melted cheese quesadillas can you eat? For many, it's endless. This is an easy to prepare option for when multiple quesadillas are required.

Serving size: 4 portions

TOTAL CALORIES: 194
Fat: 10g | Carbs: 4g | Protein: 21g

INGREDIENTS

- 350g/12.3oz beefsteak
- 4 tbsp. Worcestershire sauce
- ½ lemon, juiced
- ½ tbsp. garlic powder
- ½ tbsp. ginger powder
- 1 tbsp. olive oil
- 1 tbsp. sriracha
- 5 basil leaves
- ½ tsp. salt

INSTRUCTIONS

1. Preheat your Air Fryer to 160°C/320°F.
2. Add the Worcestershire sauce, lemon juice, garlic, ginger, olive oil, sriracha, basil leaves and salt to a blender and combine well.
3. Add the beefsteak to a cooking pan and cover it with the sauce. Cook it in the Air Fryer for 15 minutes, flipping once.
4. Cut the meat into thin slices and use it to prepare quesadillas.

BEEF STRIPS WITH CURRY

These beef strips are crunchy, tasty, and perfect for beer night.

Serving size: 3 portions

TOTAL CALORIES: 234
Fat: 7g | Carbs: 19g | Protein: 22g

INGREDIENTS

- 200g/7oz beefsteak
- ½ cup flour
- ½ cup breadcrumbs
- 1 egg
- A little milk
- 2 tbsp. curry
- ½ tsp. salt

INSTRUCTIONS

1. Cut the beefsteak into long, thin strips.
2. Combine the flour, curry and salt. Beat the eggs in a separate bowl, and in a third bowl place the breadcrumbs.
3. Take one beef strip and coat it in the flour mixture, then the egg, then the breadcrumbs. Repeat for all strips.
4. Preheat your Air Fryer to 200°C/400°F.
5. Add a little oil to the basket, then add all the beef strips and cook for 12 minutes, flipping once.

BEEF RISOTTO

You'll feel like a professional chef when you serve up this dish!

Serving size: 3 portions

TOTAL CALORIES: 432
Fat: 15g | Carbs: 52g | Protein: 21g

INGREDIENTS

- 200g/7oz beefsteak
- 2 tbsp. corn starch
- 2 tbsp. olive oil
- 4 tbsp. soy sauce
- 2 tbsp. sugar
- 2 cloves garlic
- 2 tbsp. grated garlic
- ½ tsp. salt
- 3 cups boiled rice

INSTRUCTIONS

1. Cut the steak into long, thin strips and coat each with corn starch.
2. Place the strips in the Air Fryer basket, add little oil and cook for 10 minutes at 190°C/380°F, flipping once.
3. Combine the soy sauce, sugar, garlic minced, ginger grated and salt in a saucepan and let simmer for 5 minutes.
4. When the strips are cooked, add them to the saucepan to soak for 10 minutes.
5. Serve the rice and beef strips in a bowl and enjoy.

BACON-WRAPPED BEEF STRIPS AND SPINACH

This dense meal will give you the energy you need for the rest of your day.

Serving size: 2 portions

TOTAL CALORIES: 382
Fat: 13g | Carbs: 32g | Protein: 33g

INGREDIENTS

- 200g/7oz beefsteak
- 10 slices bacon
- A handful of spinach
- ½ cup millet
- 1 cup vegetable stock
- A little oil for the cooking basket

INSTRUCTIONS

1. Preheat your Air Fryer to 200°C/400°F.
2. Prepare 10 strips of the beefsteak and wrap them in bacon.
3. Add a little oil to the basket, then add the bacon strips and cook for 10 minutes, flipping once or twice.
4. Meanwhile, cook the millet and spinach. Combine the vegetable stock, millet and spinach in a saucepan. Cover and let it simmer for 12 minutes. Serve together and enjoy.

BEEF AND VEGGIE NACHOS

The Spanish say "Me encantan los nachos" – meaning that they adore nachos. Try this recipe and you'll understand what they're talking about.

Serving size: 3 portions

TOTAL CALORIES: 232
Fat: 15g | Carbs: 13g | Protein: 10g

INGREDIENTS

- 100g/3.5oz ground beef
- 1 tbsp. tomato sauce
- 1 avocado
- 1 onion
- ½ tomato
- A little lemon juice
- 3 slices yellow cheese
- 1 tbsp. olive oil
- A pinch of salt
- 1 small bag of nacho crisps

INSTRUCTIONS

1. Preheat your Air Fryer to 200°C/400°F.
2. In a cooking pan that fits your Air Fryer, combine the beef with the tomato sauce and salt. Place it in the Air Fryer and cook for 7 minutes.
3. In a separate bowl, mash the avocado it until it is creamy. Add the chopped tomato and onion, a little salt, lemon juice and mix it well.
4. Take the beef out of the Air Fryer and add a little oil to the basket. Add the nachos, then the guacamole, cooked beef and yellow cheese on top.
5. Cook for 4 minutes and serve.

BEEF-STUFFED EGGPLANTS

This healthy lunch recipe might not be crispy, but it's certainly juicy!

Serving size: 2 portions

TOTAL CALORIES: 246
Fat: 8g | Carbs: 17g | Protein: 26g

INGREDIENTS

- 100g/3.5oz ground beef
- ½ cup rice
- 1 cup beef broth
- A little salt
- ½ onion
- 1 carrot
- 2 medium sized eggplants
- 1 cup grated mozzarella

INSTRUCTIONS

1. Dice or grate the carrot and onion. Combine with the meat, rice and beef broth. Place this mixture in a cooking pan and add it to the Air Fryer basket. Cook for 10 minutes at 180°C/360°F.
2. Cut the eggplants in half and scoop about half the filling out. Fill the holes with the meat mixture.
3. Add a little oil to the basket, then add the eggplants and cook for 10 minutes. Open the basket, sprinkle mozzarella on top of the eggplants and cook for a further 3 minutes.

GROUND BEEF PUFFED BOMBS

Sometimes, all you need is a dish that combines your favourite sauce and small, tasty beef bites.

Serving size: 4 portions

TOTAL CALORIES: 340
Fat: 21g | Carbs: 31g | Protein: 16g

INGREDIENTS

- 200g/7oz ground beef
- 2tbsp. sriracha
- ½ tsp. salt
- ½ tsp. paprika
- 1 tbsp. il
- 1 sheet puff pastry

INSTRUCTIONS

1. Preheat your Air Fryer to 200°C/400°F.
2. Combine the meat with the spices, sriracha and oil, and mix well. Add it to a cooking pan and cook it in the Air Fryer for 10 minutes.
3. Take the puff pastry and cut it into 5cm squares. In the centre of each square add 1 tbsp. meat and then form balls with the pastry.
4. Place the balls in the Air Fryer basket and cook for 10 minutes.

31 · TRADITIONAL MASHED POTATOES AND MEATLOAF

Buttery mashed potatoes coated in sauce and served with soft beef.

Serving size: 3 portions

TOTAL CALORIES: 580
Fat: 33g | Carbs: 43g | Protein: 27g

INGREDIENTS

- 3 pcs. beefsteak
- ½ cup vegetable broth
- 1 garlic clove
- ½ tsp. salt
- 1 carrot
- 3 boiled potatoes
- 1 tbsp. butter
- ½ cup milk
- A pinch of salt

INSTRUCTIONS

1. Place the beefsteaks, garlic, carrot, salt and broth in a cooking pan.
2. Place the cooking pan in the Air Fryer basket and cook for 20 minutes at 140°C/280°F. While cooking, open the basket and flip the beefsteaks once or twice.
3. Meanwhile, combine the potatoes (boiled and peeled), melted butter, milk and salt. Mash with a masher or fork, until smooth.
4. When the meat is cooked, remove it from the pan. The remaining garlic and carrot juice can be mashed or blended in a food processor.
5. Serve a base of mashed potato with the beefsteak and carrot-garlic dressing.

---

32 · ROLLED BEEF WITH MOZZARELLA

Mozzarella sits in the centre of these beef rolls – cut through their melting centres and serve alongside a side dish of your choice.

Serving size: 3 portions

TOTAL CALORIES: 258
Fat: 15g | Carbs: 3g | Protein: 34g

INGREDIENTS

- 300g/10.5oz ground beef
- 2 tbsp. tomato sauce
- 1 egg
- 2 tbsp. breadcrumbs
- ½ tsp. paprika
- ½ tsp. salt
- Two 100g/7oz slices mozzarella

INSTRUCTIONS

1. Combine the meat, tomato sauce, egg, breadcrumbs, paprika and salt. Mix well. On a flat surface, place some plastic wrap and the meat on top. Spread out until it is 2cm thick. Add the mozzarella cheese to the middle and roll the meat with the help of the plastic wrap.
2. Preheat the Air Fryer to 160°C/320°F.
3. Add a little oil to the basket, then add the meat roll and cook for 20 minutes, turning the meat three times.
4. Serve slices of the meat with any side dish of your choice.

33 MINI TAQUITOS WITH SRIRACHA

This tasty Mexican-inspired dish can be achieved with just a few core ingredients.

Serving size: 4 portions

TOTAL CALORIES: 278
Fat: 10g | Carbs: 25g | Protein: 22g

INGREDIENTS

- 350g/12.3oz ground beef
- 1 grated onion
- 1 egg
- 1 tsp. curry spice
- 1 tbsp. flour
- ½ tsp. salt
- 8 small corn tortillas
- ½ cup of sriracha
- A little oil for the cooking basket

INSTRUCTIONS

1. Combine the meat, spices, flour, egg, and onion and mix well.
2. Take one tortilla and add 1 tbsp. meat mixture. Roll the tortilla and pierce it with a wooden skewer. Repeat the process with the remaining tortillas.
3. Preheat the Air Fryer to 180°C/360°F.
4. Add a little oil to the basket, then place the taquitos in the basket and cook for 6 minutes. Open the basket and flip them, then cook for a further 3 minutes.
5. Serve with sriracha on top.

9 | MAIN DISHES WITH CHICKEN

1. Crispy fried chicken wings
2. Ultimate crispy fried chicken
3. Chicken steak and corn
4. Chilli chicken sticks
5. Chipotle chicken wings
6. Russian chicken pie
7. Honey chicken risotto
8. BBQ mashed chicken
9. Green chicken salad
10. Mexican chicken steak
11. Crispy veggies with chicken
12. Peanut butter chicken
13. Curry chicken stew
14. Beans and chicken salad
15. Cheesy fried chicken
16. Lebanese chicken strips
17. Chicken pasta
18. Soy sweet-and-sour wings
19. Juicy chicken in mushroom sauce
20. Crispy chicken burgers
21. Tortilla chicken balls
22. Chicken salad with mozzarella and rocket

DON'T FORGET TO GET THE

TOP RECIPES FROM THIS BOOK AS

A DOWNLOADABLE PDF IN COLOUR

FOR FREE!

SCAN THE QR CODE BELOW

SCAN ME

CRISPY FRIED CHICKEN WINGS

They might look like fast-food chicken wings, but these Air Fryer-cooked delights are oil-free.

Serving size: 3 portions

TOTAL CALORIES: 169

Fat: 3g | Carbs: 12g | Protein: 24g

INGREDIENTS

- 9 chicken wings
- 4 tbsp. BBQ sauce
- ½ cup corn flakes, crushed or blended

INSTRUCTIONS

1. Preheat your Air Fryer to 200°C/400°F.
2. Toss the chicken wings with BBQ sauce, then add them to a bowl with the corn flakes. Shake the bowl so that every side of the chicken wing is sufficiently covered in corn flakes.
3. Add a little oil to the basket, then add the chicken wings and cook for 12 minutes opening once to turn the chicken.

ULTIMATE CRISPY FRIED CHICKEN

This dish might not be deep-fried, but it will taste like it is! It's a quick recipe that lasts well in a lunch box.

Serving size: 2 portions

TOTAL CALORIES: 358

Fat: 6g | Carbs: 50g | Protein: 27g

INGREDIENTS

- 2 chicken steaks
- ½ cup breadcrumbs
- ½ cup flour
- 1 egg
- 1 tbsp. paprika
- 1 tsp. salt
- 1 tsp. curcuma
- A little oil for the cooking basket

INSTRUCTIONS

1. Preheat your Air Fryer to 170°C/340°F.
2. Prepare three separate bowls. In the first, mix the flour, salt and curcuma. In the second beat the egg, and in the third combine the breadcrumbs and paprika.
3. Take one chicken steak and dip it in the flour mixture, then the egg, and then the breadcrumbs.
4. Add a little oil to the basket, then add the chicken to the basket and cook for 15 minutes. Open once and flip the steak.

CHICKEN STEAK AND CORN

This crispy yet juicy dish is fast and easy to prepare. Serve it alongside a side dish of veggies or salad.

Serving size: 2 portions

TOTAL CALORIES: 229

Fat: 5g | Carbs: 20g | Protein: 27g

INGREDIENTS

- 2 chicken steaks
- ½ cup small corn flakes
- 1 egg
- ½ tsp. salt
- ½ tsp. white pepper
- ½ tsp. oregano
- A little oil for the cooking basket

INSTRUCTIONS

1. Preheat your Air Fryer to 180°C/360°F.
2. In one bowl, combine the egg with the spices and salt. Add the steaks to the bowl and let sit for 2 minutes. Then, dip the steaks in a bowl with the corn flakes.
3. Add a little oil to the basket, then add the corn steaks and cook for 14 minutes, flipping them once.

CHILLI CHICKEN STICKS

These chicken sticks are perfect for every occasion, picnic or gathering.

Serving size: 3 portions

TOTAL CALORIES: 129

Fat: 3g | Carbs: 9g | Protein: 17g

INGREDIENTS

- 2 chicken steaks
- ½ cup chilli sauce
- ½ cup breadcrumbs
- ½ tsp. paprika
- ½ tsp. salt
- 1 jalapeno pepper
- A little oil for the cooking basket

INSTRUCTIONS

1. Cut the chicken into thin strips. You should have 20 strips in total. Cover them with the chilli sauce and let them rest for 5 minutes.
2. Combine the breadcrumbs with the salt, paprika and finely chopped jalapeno pepper. Add the chicken strips and mix well.
3. Preheat your Air Fryer to 200°C/400°F.
4. Add a little oil to the basket, then add the meat strips and cook for 10 minutes, shaking once. Serve your chilli sticks and enjoy.

⑤ CHIPOTLE CHICKEN WINGS

Chipotle chicken is popular for a reason. Try this tasty and slightly modified recipe that can be prepared in less than 10 minutes.

Serving size: 3 portions

TOTAL CALORIES: 266
Fat: 17g | Carbs: 5g | Protein: 23g

INGREDIENTS

- 3 boneless, skinless chicken thighs
- 1 clove garlic
- 1 tbsp. maple syrup
- 1 scallion
- ½ tsp. salt
- 1 lime
- 2 tbsp. olive oil

INSTRUCTIONS

1. Mince the garlic and dice the scallion. Combine the maple syrup, scallion, salt, oil, lime juice and garlic, then add the chicken thighs and let them rest for 5 minutes.
2. Preheat your Air Fryer to 170°C/340°F.
3. Place the meat in a cooking pan that fits the Air Fryer and cook for 12 minutes.

RUSSIAN CHICKEN PIE ⑥

This unique recipe results in a crispy dough filled with creamy chicken.

Serving size: 4 portions

TOTAL CALORIES: 628
Fat: 38g | Carbs: 57g | Protein: 15g

INGREDIENTS

- 1 chicken steak
- ½ cup peas
- 1 carrot
- ½ cup heavy cream
- ½ cup grated mozzarella
- A pinch of salt
- A pinch of black pepper
- 2 sheets of puff pastry

INSTRUCTIONS

1. Preheat your Air Fryer to 200°C/400°F.
2. Add a little oil to the basket, then cook the chicken steak for 5 minutes.
3. Then, shred the chicken, and add the peas, chopped carrot, heavy cream, salt, pepper, and mozzarella to a bowl. Mix well.
4. Take a baking pan that fits the Air Fryer and line it with the first sheet of puff pastry. Add the chicken mixture and 'close' the pie with another sheet of puff pastry on top. Trim the extra pastry from the edges.
5. Place the pie in the Air Fryer for 12 minutes at 180°C/360°F.

HONEY CHICKEN RISOTTO

This chicken-based meal has a high nutritional value, providing carbs, protein and energy.

Serving size: 3 portions

TOTAL CALORIES: 243

Fat: 4g | Carbs: 28g | Protein: 24g

INGREDIENTS

- 1 cup rice
- 2 cups chicken broth
- 3 chicken thighs – skinless, boneless
- ½ tsp. curry powder
- 1 tbsp. honey
- 1 tbsp. soy sauce
- A pinch of salt

INSTRUCTIONS

1. Preheat your Air Fryer to 120°C/240°F.
2. Combine the chicken thighs with the honey, soy sauce, salt, and curry powder.
3. Take a cooking pan and add the rice and broth, then add the chicken thighs and extra sauce.
4. Place the pan in the Air Fryer and cook for 15 minutes. Open, stir a little then cook for a further 10 minutes on 180°C/360°F.

BBQ MASHED CHICKEN

This sweet and salty dish can be served with mashed potato or bowl of quinoa, but it's the BBQ sauce that brings the magic.

Serving size: 3 portions

TOTAL CALORIES: 404

Fat: 3g | Carbs: 5g | Protein: 15g

INGREDIENTS

- 2 chicken steaks
- 4 tbsp. BBQ sauce
- ½ tsp. paprika
- A pinch of salt
- ½ tsp. black pepper
- A little oil for the cooking basket

INSTRUCTIONS

1. Preheat your Air Fryer to 120°C/240°F.
2. Add a little oil to the basket, then add the chicken steaks and cook for 7 minutes.
3. Add the steak to a bowl and shred it into small pieces. Combine it with the BBQ sauce, spices and salt.
4. Place the mixture in a cooking pan and cook it in the Air Fryer for 10 minutes at 180°C/360°F. Serve on burger buns or with mashed potatoes.

GREEN CHICKEN SALAD

Combine veggies with broccoli, a little basil and chicken, and you've got a perfect meal.

Serving size: 3 portions

TOTAL CALORIES: 207
Fat: 3g | Carbs: 28g | Protein: 17g

iNGREDiENTS

- 2 chicken steaks
- 2 cups fresh broccoli
- ½ cup Caesar sauce
- ½ white onion
- A pinch of salt
- ½ cucumber
- A little fresh thyme
- 3 pita breads – optional

iNSTRUCTiONS

1. Preheat your Air Fryer to 200°C/400°F.
2. Add a little oil to the basket, then place the chicken in the Air Fryer and cook for 10 minutes, flipping once.
3. Chop the broccoli into small pieces. Shred the chicken and add to the broccoli. Then slice the cucumber and add it to the salad, alongside the Caesar sauce, chopped onion and salt. Toss the salad and sprinkle with thyme.
4. Serve with pita bread.

MEXICAN CHICKEN STEAK

The tomato sauce is the star of this dish, and it pairs perfectly with the chicken.

Serving size: 2 portions

TOTAL CALORIES: 213
Fat: 8g | Carbs: 12g | Protein: 23g

iNGREDiENTS

- 2 chicken steaks
- A handful of basil
- 2 minced garlic cloves
- 4 tbsp. tomato sauce
- 1 tbsp. sugar
- ½ tsp. salt
- 1 tsp. olive oil

iNSTRUCTiONS

1. Combine the minced garlic, sugar, oil, tomato sauce, salt and basil. Mix well.
2. Take a cooking pan that fits the Air Fryer and place the chicken steak in it. Add the tomato sauce mixture and cook for 15 minutes at 160°C/320°F, mixing once.

CRISPY VEGGIES WITH CHICKEN

An easy combination of Mediterranean veggies and soft chicken.

Serving size: 2 portions

TOTAL CALORIES: 285
Fat: 16g | Carbs: 14g | Protein 23g

INGREDIENTS

- 2 chicken steaks
- 2 red peppers
- 2 carrots
- 1 tomato
- 1 tsp. curcuma
- ½ tsp. garlic powder
- ½ tsp. salt
- 2 tbsp. olive oil

INSTRUCTIONS

1. Cut the peppers into slices, then cut the chicken, carrots and tomato into thin strips.
2. Place the ingredients in a cooking pan and add the spices, salt and oil. Mix well.
3. Cook on 140°C/280°F for 15 minutes, mixing once.
4. Serve alone or on pita bread.

PEANUT BUTTER CHICKEN

Serve this dish with warm bread and you'll definitely go back for seconds!

Serving size: 3 portions

TOTAL CALORIES: 276
Fat: 16g | Carbs: 7g | Protein: 31g

INGREDIENTS

- 3 chicken steaks
- 1 cup heavy cream
- 3 tbsp. peanut butter
- ½ tsp. salt
- ½ tsp. black pepper
- ½ tsp. dried basil
- 5-6 cherry tomatoes

INSTRUCTIONS

1. Preheat your Air Fryer to 180°C/360°F.
2. Add a little oil to the basket, then add the steak and cook for 7 minutes.
3. Preheat a saucepan then add the heavy cream, peanut butter, salt, black pepper, and dried basil. Let it simmer, then mix well and place it to the side.
4. Open the Air Fryer basket and place the meat, sauce and tomatoes in a cooking pan. Cook for 5 minutes.

CURRY CHICKEN STEW

This chicken stew sits at the top of the tasty recipes list, and can also be prepared with beef.

Serving size: 4 portions

TOTAL CALORIES: 145
Fat: 3g | Carbs: 17g | Protein: 14g

INGREDIENTS

- 2 chicken thighs, skinless and boneless
- 2 cups chicken broth
- ½ cup millet
- 1 carrot
- 1 cup small potatoes
- A little garlic powder
- A pinch of black pepper
- ½ tbsp. salt

INSTRUCTIONS

1. Cut the potatoes in half, slice the carrot, and cube the chicken thighs.
2. Add them to a cooking pan that fits the Air Fryer, then add the rest of the ingredients.
3. Cook for 20 minutes on 100°C/200°F, opening once or twice to mix the stew.

BEANS AND CHICKEN SALAD

Some days you just need a light meal – but it can still be tasty!

Serving size: 3 portions

TOTAL CALORIES: 130
Fat: 4g | Carbs: 6g | Protein: 19g

INGREDIENTS

- 100g/3.5oz fresh young snow peas
- 2 chicken steaks
- 1 tbsp. pesto
- 1 tbsp. low-fat mayo
- ½ zucchini
- 1 tomato
- 1 cucumber
- A pinch of salt

INSTRUCTIONS

1. Preheat the Air Fryer to 160°C/320°F.
2. Add a little oil to the basket, then add the chicken and cook for 10 minutes, flipping the meat once.
3. Prepare the salad. Cut all the veggies into small pieces, then combine in a bowl. Shred the chicken and add it to the bowl. Dress the salad with mayo and pesto, then sprinkle with salt and mix it well.

CHEESY FRIED CHICKEN

This dish sees chicken filled with melted cheese and fried without oil – perfection.

Serving size: 2 portions

TOTAL CALORIES:257

Fat: 8g | Carbs: 14g | Protein: 31g

INGREDIENTS

- 2 chicken breasts
- 2 slices cheddar cheese
- 2 slices blue cheese
- 1 egg
- 2 tbsp. flour
- 2 tbsp. breadcrumbs
- A little salt
- 1 tsp. smoked paprika
- A little oil for the cooking basket

INSTRUCTIONS

1. Cut a pocket in the chicken breast. It should be a horizontal cut that will provide space for the cheese filling.
2. Fill the chicken with one slice of cheddar and one slice of blue cheese.
3. Place the flour in one bowl, beat the egg in another, and combine the breadcrumbs with smoked paprika in a third.
4. Dip the meat in the flour, then the egg, followed by the breadcrumbs.
5. Preheat the Air Fryer to 180°C/360°F.
6. Add a little oil to the basket, then add the chicken to the basket and cook for 10 minutes, flipping once.

LEBANESE CHICKEN STRIPS

These chicken strips are traditionally deep-fried, but fry them in an Air Fryer instead and the flavour will be even more enticing.

Serving size: 3 portions

TOTAL CALORIES:280

Fat: 11g | Carbs: 23g | Protein: 21g

INGREDIENTS

- 2 chicken steaks
- ¼ tsp. salt
- ½ cup flour
- ½ cup coconut flakes
- 2 eggs
- ½ cup milk
- A little oil for the cooking basket

INSTRUCTIONS

1. Cut the chicken steaks into strips.
2. Combine the flour and salt in one bowl, and in another combine the egg and milk. Place the coconut flakes in a third bowl.
3. Place the chicken strips in the first bowl and cover them with flour, then dip one strip in the egg mixture, followed by the coconut flakes. Repeat this process with all the strips.
4. Preheat your Air Fryer to 200°C/400°F.
5. Add a little oil to the basket, then add the coconut strips to the basket and cook for 12 minutes. Open twice to shake and twist them a little.

THE AIR FRYER COOKBOOK FOR BEGINNERS

CHICKEN PASTA

An Italian-inspired recipe featuring chicken, spinach and brussels sprouts.

Serving size: 4 portions

TOTAL CALORIES: 250
Fat: 5g | Carbs: 35g | Protein: 16g

INGREDIENTS

- 200g/7oz ground white chicken
- 1 cup brussels sprouts
- A handful of baby spinach
- ½ tsp. garlic powder
- ¼ tsp. salt
- 1 tbsp. olive oil
- 400g/14.1oz cooked fusilli

INSTRUCTIONS

1. Preheat your Air Fryer to 200°C/400°F.
2. In a cooking pan that fits the Air Fryer, combine the ground chicken, brussels sprouts, baby spinach, garlic, salt and oil. Mix well and cook for 10 minutes.
3. Combine the cooked pasta with the cooked chicken.

SOY SWEET-AND-SOUR WINGS

This recipe can be a little sticky but add a little fresh lime and you're sorted.

Serving size: 3 portions

TOTAL CALORIES: 163
Fat: 4g | Carbs: 10g | Protein: 23g

INGREDIENTS

- 9 chicken wings
- 2 tbsp. maple syrup
- 1 tbsp. grated ginger
- 1 clove minced garlic
- 2 tbsp. soy sauce
- ¼ tsp. salt
- A pinch of pepper
- 1 lime

INSTRUCTIONS

1. Preheat your Air Fryer to 200°C/400°F.
2. Combine all ingredients in one bowl, then let the chicken wings rest in the marinade for 20 minutes.
3. Add a little oil to the basket, then place the chicken wings in the basket and cook for 10 minutes.

JUICY CHICKEN IN MUSHROOM SAUCE

(IN MINUTES)
PREP **15**
COOK **22**

Caramelized onions and mushrooms are a perfect combination. This sauce is a must for spring-inspired cooking.

Serving size: 2 portions

TOTAL CALORIES: 340
Fat: 15g | Carbs: 23g | Protein: 27g

INGREDIENTS

- 2 onions
- 2 tbsp. sugar
- 1 cup white mushrooms
- 2 chicken steaks
- 1 tbsp. butter
- ½ cup heavy cream
- ½ tsp. garlic powder
- ¼ tsp. salt

INSTRUCTIONS

1. Slice the onions into thin half-moon slices. Toss them with sugar then add them to the Air Fryer basket.
2. Cook for 10 minutes at 180°C/360°F.
3. Take a cooking pan that fits the Air Fryer and add the chicken steaks, chopped mushrooms, caramelised onions, butter, heavy cream, garlic powder and salt. Mix a little, then cook for 12 minutes.

CRISPY CHICKEN BURGERS

(IN MINUTES)
PREP **10**
COOK **12**

All children love chicken burgers – and this healthier air-fried version is no exception!

Serving size: 2 portions

TOTAL CALORIES: 304
Fat: 3g | Carbs: 33g | Protein: 27g

INGREDIENTS

- 2 chicken steaks
- 2 tbsp. mustard
- 4 pickles
- 2 slices yellow cheese
- 2 tbsp. tomato sauce
- 2 lettuce leaves
- 2 burger buns

INSTRUCTIONS

1. Preheat your Air Fryer to 200°C/400°F.
2. Spread mustard over the chicken steaks then place it in the Air Fryer basket. Cook for 10 minutes, checking once to flip the meat.
3. Cut the burger buns in half, then spread a little tomato sauce and add a chicken steak, sliced pickles and one slice of yellow cheese. Close the burgers.
4. Add them to the basket and cook for a further 2 minutes.

TORTILLA CHICKEN BALLS

Meatballs don't always have to feature beef – and these chicken balls are perfect in a tortilla with salad.

Serving size: 3 portions

TOTAL CALORIES: 227
Fat: 5g | Carbs: 25g | Protein: 21g

INGREDIENTS

- 200g/7oz ground chicken
- 1 egg
- 2 tbsp. breadcrumbs
- ¼ tsp. salt
- A little pepper
- ½ cup grated cheddar cheese
- 2 tomatoes
- ½ cabbage
- 3 tbsp. sweet chilli sauce
- 3 tortillas

INSTRUCTIONS

1. Combine the meat, eggs, breadcrumbs, salt, pepper and cheddar cheese. Mix well, then form eight balls.
2. Preheat your Air Fryer to 160°C/320°F.
3. Add baking paper to the basket and place the chicken balls inside. Cook for 10 minutes, shaking once or twice.
4. Take the tortilla, spread a little sweet chilli sauce over it and add 2-3 meatballs. Wrap it like a burrito and serve with the salad.

CHICKEN SALAD WITH MOZZARELLA AND ROCKET

This meal is light, high in protein and tasty – what more could you ask for?

Serving size: 2 portions

TOTAL CALORIES: 683
Fat: 52g | Carbs: 21g | Protein: 27g

INGREDIENTS

- 1 chicken steak
- 100g/3.5oz mozzarella
- A handful of rocket
- ½ cup walnuts
- ½ cup cooked quinoa
- ½ lemon, juiced
- A pinch of salt
- 2 tbsp. olive oil

INSTRUCTIONS

1. Preheat your Air Fryer to 200°C/400°F.
2. Add a little oil to the basket, then add the chicken steak and cook for 10 minutes, turning once.
3. Combine the rocket, slices of mozzarella, cooked quinoa and walnuts. Cut the chicken into thin strips and add it to the salad. Dress it with lemon juice and olive oil, then sprinkle with salt.

10 | MAIN DISHES WITH PORK

1. Bacon and tomato risotto
2. Pork frittata
3. Crispy pork tender rinds
4. Pork steak with potato
5. Pork sausages and mixed beans
6. Italian pork pizza
7. Pork vindaloo
8. Stuffed pork peppers
9. Mexican pork carnitas
10. Crispy pork chops
11. Shredded pork in a sweet sauce
12. Garlic pork chops
13. Pork and millet stew
14. BBQ pork ribs
15. Pork burrito
16. Cooked pita pork loin
17. Pork chops with beans and onions
18. Mushroom pork stew
19. Crunchy veggies and bacon
20. Pork noodle soup
21. Toasted pork steak sandwich
22. Shredded pork burgers
23. Keto pork steak with almond sauce

DON'T FORGET TO GET THE

TOP RECIPES FROM THIS BOOK AS

A DOWNLOADABLE PDF IN COLOUR

FOR FREE!

SCAN THE QR CODE BELOW

BACON AND TOMATO RISOTTO

A quick, simple and easy to prepare lunch.

Serving size: 4 portions

TOTAL CALORIES: 462
Fat: 32g | Carbs: 18g | Protein: 25g

INGREDIENTS

- 6 slices bacon
- 1 cup rice
- 2 cups veggie broth
- 1 cup veggies (peas, carrots, cauliflower)
- 2 tbsp. butter
- 1 tbsp. coconut oil
- ½ tsp. salt
- ½ tsp. curry powder
- 1 onion

INSTRUCTIONS

1. Cut the bacon into small cubes. Cut the onion into thin slices. Melt the butter.
2. Take a cooking pan that fits the Air Fryer and add the onion and butter.
3. Preheat your Air Fryer to 200°C/400°F.
4. Cook the onion for 5 minutes. Take the pan out of the Air Fryer and add the rest of the ingredients.
5. Lower the temperature to 150°C/300°F and place the cooking pan back in the basket. Cook for 12 minutes.

PORK FRITTATA

: This delicious frittata can be served with a slice of bread or a small bowl of salad.

Serving size: 4 portions

TOTAL CALORIES: 174
Fat: 8g | Carbs: 6g | Protein: 20g

INGREDIENTS

- 200g/7oz pork
- 5 eggs
- 2 tbsp. cornmeal
- 1 tbsp. BBQ sauce
- ½ cup broccoli
- ¼ tsp. salt
- A pinch of pepper

INSTRUCTIONS

1. Preheat your Air Fryer to 160°C/320°F.
2. Add a little oil to the basket, then add the pork to the basket and cook for 10 minutes, flipping it once.
3. Shred the cooked pork, then combine with eggs, broccoli, cornmeal, salt and pepper. Mix the ingredients well.
4. Place them in a cooking pan and cook for 10 minutes.

CRISPY PORK TENDER RINDS

Crispy pork rind isn't always easy to achieve, but the secret is revealed in this recipe.

Serving size: 4 portions

TOTAL CALORIES: 250
Fat: 16g | Carbs: 1g | Protein: 25g

INGREDIENTS

- 500g/17.6oz pork rinds
- 1 tbsp. mustard
- 1 tbsp. butter
- Salt, to taste
- Black pepper, to taste

INSTRUCTIONS

1. Spread mustard over the pork rinds. Add butter to the skin.
2. Preheat your Air Fryer to its maximum temperature.
3. Place the large piece of meat in the basket and cook for 7 minutes on maximum heat. Then, lower the heat to 180°C/360°F and cook for a further 10 minutes.
4. Remove the meat from the Air Fryer and cut it into four even pieces.

PORK STEAK WITH POTATO

A slightly modified version of a classic recipe prepared in the Air Fryer.

Serving size: 2 portions

TOTAL CALORIES: 426
Fat: 18g | Carbs: 44g | Protein: 25g

INGREDIENTS

- 2 pork steaks
- 2 large sweet potatoes
- 2 tbsp. olive oil
- ½ tsp. salt
- A pinch of pepper
- 1 tbsp. tomato paste

INSTRUCTIONS

1. Cut the potatoes into long, thick strips. Toss them with salt, tomato sauce, olive oil and pepper. Add a little salt and oil to the meat.
2. Preheat your Air Fryer to 160°C/320°F.
3. Add a little oil to the basket, then add the potatoes and steak and cook for 15 minutes, flipping the meat and shaking the basket once.

THE AIR FRYER COOKBOOK FOR BEGINNERS

PORK SAUSAGES AND MIXED BEANS

You can buy these sausages at your nearest butcher – ask for the semi-raw pork sausages.

Serving size: 3 portions

TOTAL CALORIES: 338
Fat: 21g | Carbs: 19g | Protein: 18g

INGREDIENTS

- 3 pork sausages
- ½ cup guacamole
- 1 cup canned black beans
- 2 tbsp. sriracha
- A pinch of salt
- 1 tomato
- A little oil for the cooking basket

INSTRUCTIONS

1. Preheat your Air Fryer to 200°C/400°F.
2. Add a little oil to the basket, then place the sausages inside and cook for 7 minutes, flipping them once
3. Combine the guacamole with the canned beans and chopped tomatoes. Add a little salt. Slice the sausages and add them to the top of the guacamole mixture.

ITALIAN PORK PIZZA

Pork is a soft flavour on pizza, and this is the perfect blend of tomatoes, meat and cheese.

Serving size: 1 pizza

TOTAL CALORIES: 640
Fat: 22g | Carbs: 58g | Protein: 55g

INGREDIENTS

- 2 thin, salted pork ribs
- 1 Air Fryer pizza base
- 2 tbsp. tomato sauce for pizza
- 100g/3.5oz mozzarella
- ½ tsp. oregano

INSTRUCTIONS

1. Preheat your Air Fryer to 200°C/400°F.
2. Cut the pork ribs into small squares. Add the tomato sauce to the pizza base, then the pork chops and mozzarella slices. Sprinkle with oregano.
3. Place the pizza in the Air Fryer basket and cook for a maximum of 8 minutes.

PORK VINDALOO

This Indian dish is spicy but tasty – you won't believe it contains meat!

Serving size: 3 portions

TOTAL CALORIES: 210
Fat: 13g | Carbs: 1g | Protein: 22g

INGREDIENTS

- 300g/10.5oz pork loin cubes
- 2 tbsp. olive oil
- 1 tsp. curry powder
- ½ tsp. paprika
- ½ tsp. black pepper
- ¼ tsp. salt
- ½ cup veggie broth

INSTRUCTIONS

1. Preheat your Air Fryer to 160°C/320°F.
2. In a cooking pan, mix all the ingredients together then cook for 10 minutes. Open the basket, mix well and cook for a further 10 minutes.

STUFFED PORK PEPPERS

Bell peppers are perfect for stuffing and the end result always looks fabulous.

Serving size: 4 portions

TOTAL CALORIES: 237
Fat: 4g | Carbs: 26g | Protein: 21g

INGREDIENTS

- 4 bell peppers
- 300g/10.5oz ground pork
- 1 cup rice
- 1 cup tomato puree
- 1 potato
- ½ onion
- ½ tsp. salt
- ½ tsp. paprika

INSTRUCTIONS

1. Dice the onion, then combine with the ground pork, rice, tomato puree, salt, pepper and paprika.
2. Cut away the pepper stalks and remove the seeds. Stuff every pepper with the mixture pork mixture. Slice the potato and add one slice to every pepper – this protects and seals them.
3. Preheat your Air Fryer to 140°C/280°F.
4. Add the peppers to the basket and cook for 18 minutes.

THE AIR FRYER COOKBOOK FOR BEGINNERS

MEXICAN PORK CARNITAS

This dish can be made with a variety of veggies. Here, it features tomato, avocado and green peppers, the classic Mexican palate.

Serving size: 2 portions

TOTAL CALORIES: 180
Fat: 5g | Carbs: 10g | Protein: 23g

INGREDIENTS

- 200g/7oz pork tenderloin
- 1 avocado
- 2 red peppers
- 2 tomatoes
- A handful of parsley
- ½ white onion
- 1 tbsp. BBQ sauce
- A pinch of salt

INSTRUCTIONS

1. Preheat your Air Fryer to 200°C/400°F.
2. Cut the meat into very small cubes. Toss them with BBQ sauce and a little salt.
3. Add a little oil to the basket, then add the meat and cook for 10 minutes, shaking the basket once throughout.
4. Slice the avocado. Combine the chopped tomatoes, onions and parsley. Serve them next to the avocado, then add the pork and thinly cut strips of red pepper.

CRISPY PORK CHOPS

These pork chops are sweet yet crispy – it's Air Fryer magic.

Serving size: 3 portions

TOTAL CALORIES: 162
Fat: 8g | Carbs: 6g | Protein: 8g

INGREDIENTS

- 12 baby ribs
- 1 tbsp. honey
- 1 tbsp. mustard
- A pinch of salt
- A little oil for the cooking basket

INSTRUCTIONS

1. Preheat your Air Fryer to 200°C/400°F.
2. Ensure you have 12 small rib pieces. Combine them with the honey, mustard and salt.
3. Add a little oil to the basket, then add the meat and cook for 12 minutes. Open the basket once to flip the ribs.

SHREDDED PORK IN A SWEET SAUCE

This pork dish is perfect for a quick sandwich or when served with potato chips.

Serving size: 3 portions

TOTAL CALORIES: 185
Fat: 9g | Carbs: 5g | Protein: 22g

INGREDIENTS

- 300g/10.5oz pork loin
- 1 tbsp. date syrup
- 1 tbsp. butter
- 1 tbsp. soy sauce
- 1 tsp. minced ginger
- A pinch of salt

INSTRUCTIONS

1. Preheat your Air Fryer to 140°C/280°F.
2. Add a little oil to the basket, then add the pork and cook for 14 minutes, turning the meat 2-3 times throughout.
3. Take the meat out of the basket and shred it. Combine the shredded meat with the date syrup, melted butter, soy sauce, minced garlic and salt. Mix well.
4. In a cooking pan that fits the Air Fryer, add the meat mixture and cook for 10 minutes on 180°C/360°F.

GARLIC PORK CHOPS

These juicy pork chops in a smooth sauce are an excellent lunch option.

Serving size: 2 portions

TOTAL CALORIES: 259
Fat: 10g | Carbs: 17g | Protein: 23g

INGREDIENTS

- 2 pork chops
- 1 tbsp. tomato paste
- 1 tbsp. mustard
- 1 tbsp. BBQ sauce
- 1 tbsp. sugar
- 1 tbsp. corn starch
- ½ tsp. black pepper
- ½ tsp. onion powder
- ¼ tsp. garlic powder
- ¼ tsp. salt
- ½ cup veggie broth

INSTRUCTIONS

1. Combine all ingredients in one bowl: tomato paste, mustard, BBQ sauce, sugar, corn starch, black pepper, onion powder, garlic powder, salt and veggie broth. Then, add the pork chops and let sit for 5 minutes.
2. Preheat your Air Fryer to 160°C/320°F.
3. Transfer the pork chop mixture to a cooking pan that fits your Air Fryer. Cook for 15 minutes, flipping the meat once.

THE AIR FRYER COOKBOOK FOR BEGINNERS

PORK AND MILLET STEW

An incredibly tasty Asian-inspired dish.

Serving size: 3 portions

TOTAL CALORIES: 247

Fat: 3g | Carbs: 33g | Protein: 24g

INGREDIENTS

- 200g/7oz ground pork
- 1 cup millet
- 1 ½ cup veggie stock
- 1 tbsp. soy sauce
- 2 tbsp. lime juice
- ½ tsp. salt
- ½ tsp. curry powder
- ½ tsp. onion powder
- Parsley, for decoration

INSTRUCTIONS

1. Combine all the ingredients in a cooking pan that fits the Air Fryer.
2. Preheat your Air Fryer to 140°C/280°F.
3. Add the cooking pan to the basket and cook for 15 minutes, checking once or twice throughout.

BBQ PORK RIBS

This recipe will bring back memories of BBQ weekends with friends – but all you need is an Air Fryer!

Serving size: 3 portions

TOTAL CALORIES: 212

Fat: 9g | Carbs: 7g | Protein: 27g

INGREDIENTS

- 400g/14.1oz pork ribs
- 4 tbsp. BBQ sauce
- 4 slice yellow cheese
- 1 tsp. onion powder
- A little salt, to taste

INSTRUCTIONS

1. Preheat your Air Fryer to 190°C/380°F.
2. Place the pork ribs on aluminium foil. Add BBQ sauce and spread it over the ribs. Then, add the onion powder and salt. Finally, add the yellow cheese on top and fold the aluminium foil around the ribs.
3. Place the foil-covered ribs in the Air Fryer basket and cook for 20 minutes. Take the meat out of the basket, open the foil and serve.

PORK BURRITO

A healthy burrito full of protein, healthy carbs and vitamins.

Serving size: 2 portions

TOTAL CALORIES: 530

Fat: 8g | Carbs: 80g | Protein: 35g

INGREDIENTS

- 200g/7oz pork loin
- 2 tortillas
- 1 cup cooked quinoa
- 1 tbsp. sriracha
- 1 tbsp. mayonnaise
- 2 tbsp. sour cream
- 1 scallion
- 1 carrot
- 2 lettuce leaves
- A pinch of salt

INSTRUCTIONS

1. Preheat your Air Fryer to 200°C/400°F.
2. Cut the pork loin into small cubes, add a little salt and place in the Air Fryer basket. Cook for 10 minutes, shaking once or twice throughout.
3. Combine the mayonnaise, sour cream, chopped scallion, sriracha and salt.
4. Add the lettuce, pork, cooked quinoa, and chopped carrot to the tortillas, then dress them with the mayonnaise mixture. Wrap them like a burrito and cook for 3 minutes.

COOKED PITA PORK LOIN

In this fast and light meal, pita bread is garnished with delicious pork loin.

Serving size: 2 portions

TOTAL CALORIES: 432

Fat: 18g | Carbs: 35g | Protein: 33g

INGREDIENTS

- 200g/7oz pork loin
- 1 cup broccoli
- 1 onion
- 1 tbsp. sesame seeds
- 2 tbsp. soy sauce
- 1 tsp. paprika
- ½ cup grated parmesan
- 2 pita breads

INSTRUCTIONS

1. Preheat your Air Fryer to 160°C/320°F.
2. Cut the onion into thin slices, then cut the broccoli into small pieces. Combine the pork loin, broccoli, onion, soy sauce, sesame seeds, and paprika in a cooking pan. Mix well.
3. Add the cooking pan to the Air Fryer basket and cook for 15 minutes, stirring once.
4. Serve one piece of pork with veggies and a pita bread. Sprinkle it with grated parmesan and enjoy.

PORK CHOPS WITH BEANS AND ONIONS

Here, the unique pork flavour penetrates beans for a rich, delicious dish.

Serving size: 2 portions

TOTAL CALORIES: 472
Fat: 11g | Carbs: 55g | Protein: 38g

INGREDIENTS

- 1 cup rice
- 1 cup canned black beans
- 2 pork chops
- 2 onions
- 1 ½ cup veggie broth
- A pinch of salt
- 1 tbsp. butter
- A little oil for the cooking basket

INSTRUCTIONS

1. Preheat your Air Fryer to 200°C/400°F.
2. Add a little oil to the basket. Cut the onions into thin rings and place them in the basket. Cook for 7 minutes.
3. Take a cooking pan and combine the rice, beans, veggie broth, salt and cooked onion. Mix well, then cook in the Air Fryer for 15 minutes at 120°C/240°F.
4. Once the beans are ready, remove them from the basket, let them cool a little, then add oil to the basket again. Add the pork chops, sprinkle a little salt on them and add a little butter on the top. Cook for 12 minutes.
5. Serve the veggies and pork chop in a bowl.

MUSHROOM PORK STEW

Try out this new recipe and discover a mouth-watering dish featuring wild mushrooms and heavy cream.

Serving size: 3 portions

TOTAL CALORIES: 179
Fat: 6g | Carbs: 5g | Protein: 25g

INGREDIENTS

- 3 pork steaks
- 2 cups wild mushrooms
- ½ cup heavy cream
- 2 minced garlic cloves
- ½ tsp. salt

INSTRUCTIONS

1. Thinly slice the mushrooms.
2. Take a cooking pan and combine the mushrooms with the minced garlic, salt and heavy cream. Add the pork steaks and coat well.
3. Preheat your Air Fryer to 140°C/280°F.
4. Place the cooking pan in the basket and cook for 18 minutes, turning the meat once.

CRUNCHY VEGGIES AND BACON

Get crispy bacon with no effort at all and enjoy a stress-free meal.

Serving size: 2 portions

TOTAL CALORIES: 406

Fat: 15g | Carbs: 39g | Protein: 29g

INGREDIENTS

- 1 cup young potatoes
- 1 cup baby carrots
- 4 slices fresh bacon
- Salt, to taste
- Black pepper, to taste
- Paprika, to taste
- A little oil for the cooking basket

INSTRUCTIONS

1. Combine the potatoes with the carrots, spices and salt.
2. Preheat your Air Fryer to 200°C/400°F.
3. Add a little oil to the basket. On one side of the basket place the bacon and sprinkle salt on it. On the other side, add the veggies. Cook for 10 minutes.
4. Take the bacon out of the basket and cook the veggies for a further 3 minutes.

PORK NOODLE SOUP

A warm bowl of noodles full of juicy pork.

Serving size: 4 portions

TOTAL CALORIES: 135

Fat: 2g | Carbs: 17g | Protein: 12g

INGREDIENTS

- 100g/3.5oz pork
- 2 mini packages noodles
- 2 cups veggie broth
- 1 tbsp. soy sauce
- ½ tsp. grated ginger
- ¼ tsp. salt
- 1 cup of broccoli

INSTRUCTIONS

1. Cut the pork into very small cubes. Combine it with the salt, soy sauce, ginger and let it sit for 5 minutes.
2. Preheat your Air Fryer to 200°C/400°F.
3. Add the meat to a cooking pan and cook it in the Air Fryer for 5 minutes.
4. Remove the meat and to the same pan add the noodles, broccoli and veggie broth.
5. Cook for a further 8 minutes at 150°C/300°F.

TOASTED PORK STEAK SANDWICH

(IN MINUTES)
PREP 15
COOK 17

Some say a good sandwich is nourishment for the soul – try this recipe and it's likely you'll agree!

Serving size: 2 portions

TOTAL CALORIES: 347
Fat: 8g | Carbs: 43g | Protein: 25g

INGREDIENTS

- 2 pork steaks
- 2 tbsp. BBQ sauce
- 1 tsp. paprika
- 1 tsp. thyme
- A pinch of salt
- A couple of eggplant slices
- 2 slices blue cheese
- 4 slices sourdough bread
- Butter, for spreading

INSTRUCTIONS

1. Place the pork steaks in a bowl and combine with the BBQ sauce, paprika, thyme and salt.
2. Preheat your Air Fryer to 200°C/400°F.
3. Add the steaks to the basket and cook for 12 minutes, turning the meat once.
4. Spread a little butter over the bread, then add the steak, blue cheese and eggplant. Sandwich the fillings and place them in the Air Fryer for 5 minutes.

SHREDDED PORK BURGERS

(IN MINUTES)
PREP 10
COOK 22

A unique mixture of cabbage, sour cream and pork served with crispy bread.

Serving size: 2 portions

TOTAL CALORIES: 329
Fat: 9g | Carbs: 37g | Protein: 22g

INGREDIENTS

- 150g/4.6oz pork
- A little oil for the cooking basket
- A pinch of salt
- 1 cup sour cream
- 100g/3.5oz cabbage
- 1tbsp. mayonnaise
- 1 tsp. curcuma
- 2 burger buns

INSTRUCTIONS

1. Preheat your Air Fryer to 160°C/320°F.
2. Add the chicken and a little bit of oil to the Air Fryer and cook for 18 minutes. Turn the meat twice.
3. Shred the pork, then mix with the sour cream, mayonnaise, chopped cabbage, curcuma and salt.
4. Form two burger patties from the pork mixture.
5. Cook them in the Air Fryer basket for 5 minutes.

(23) KETO PORK STEAK WITH ALMOND SAUCE

(IN MINUTES)

PREP
10

COOK
15

Almond sauce is naturally creamy and tasty and is best served with a soft slice of bread.

Serving size: 3 portions

TOTAL CALORIES: 369
Fat: 23g | Carbs: 7g | Protein: 27g

INGREDIENTS

- 3 pork loins
- 100g almonds
- 200ml water
- 1 garlic clove
- ½ onion
- ½ tsp. salt
- A little oil for the cooking basket

INSTRUCTIONS

1. Preheat your Air Fryer to 200°C/400°F.
2. Add a little oil to the basket, then add the pork loins and cook for 10 minutes. Flip them once.
3. In a food blender, combine the almonds, garlic, onion, salt and water. Blend until smooth.
4. Take a cooking pan that fits the Air Fryer and add the pork loins and sauce, then cook for 5 minutes.
5. Serve with a nice slice of bread.

11 | MAIN VEGAN DISHES

1. Air-fried tofu cubes
2. Pickle sticks
3. Crunchy legume potato balls
4. Air-fried veggie rolls
5. Protein veggie balls
6. Easy falafel tortillas
7. Millet cake fries
8. Vegan cheese balls
9. Deep-fried tempeh salad
10. Black bean burgers
11. Cauliflower & mushroom risotto
12. Mexican chickpea stew
13. Stuffed veggie and nuts pasta shells
14. Creamy vegan pizza
15. Vegan kebab tacos
16. Hummus potatoes
17. Veggie meatball pasta
18. Cauliflower lentils stew
19. Almond meat salad
20. Soy Bolognese pasta
21. Mushroom pie
22. Spicy tikka masala

DON'T FORGET TO GET THE

TOP RECIPES FROM THIS BOOK AS

A DOWNLOADABLE PDF IN COLOUR

FOR FREE!

SCAN THE QR CODE BELOW

SCAN ME

AIR-FRIED TOFU CUBES

The perfect recipe for crispy, air-fried tofu.

Serving size: 4 portions

TOTAL CALORIES: 258
Fat: 4g | Carbs: 45g | Protein: 12g

INGREDIENTS

- 300g/10.5oz tofu
- ½ cup corn starch
- ½ cup almond milk
- 1 cup blended corn flakes
- ½ tsp. garlic powder
- ½ tsp. chilli powder
- ½ tsp. black pepper
- ½ tsp. salt

INSTRUCTIONS

1. Cut the tofu into squares. Place the corn starch in a bowl, then place the almond milk in another. In a third bowl, combine the corn flakes, spices and salt.
2. Take one tofu cube and toss it in the corn starch, then the almond milk, and finally in the corn flake mixture.
3. Preheat your Air Fryer to 200°C/400°F.
4. Add a little oil to the basket, then add the tofu cubes and cook for 10 minutes, flipping the tofu once.

PICKLE STICKS

Yes, pickles can be an enjoyable meal! They're light but yummy, and best served with vegan cheese slices.

Serving size: 4 portions

TOTAL CALORIES: 97
Fat: 1g | Carbs: 18g | Protein: 4g

INGREDIENTS

- 12 medium-large pickles
- ½ cup flour
- ½ tsp. garlic powder
- ½ tsp. ginger powder
- ½ tsp. paprika
- ½ tsp. salt
- 4 tbsp. soda water
- 4 slices vegan cheese

INSTRUCTIONS

1. Preheat your Air Fryer to 200°C/400°F.
2. Combine the flour, spices and soda water in a bowl. Toss the pickle to the mixture, taking care to ensure that all sides are well covered. Repeat for all pickles.
3. Place the pickles in the Air Fryer basket and cook for 10 minutes. Open the basket and place the vegan cheese on top, then cook for a further 3 minutes. Serve with a dip of your choice and enjoy.

THE AIR FRYER COOKBOOK FOR BEGINNERS

CRUNCHY LEGUME POTATO BALLS

Vegan balls are an excellent source of protein and fibre and can be eaten as a regular everyday meal.

Serving size: 3 portions

TOTAL CALORIES: 264
Fat: 7g | Carbs: 35g | Protein: 16g

INGREDIENTS

- 1 cup black beans
- 2 tbsp. sunflower seeds
- 3 tbsp. oat flakes
- 2 tbsp. BBQ sauce
- 2 tbsp. water
- ¼ tsp. salt
- 1 tsp. curry powder
- ½ cup breadcrumbs

INSTRUCTIONS

1. Combine all ingredients (except the breadcrumbs) in a blender. Blend until homogenized. Place the breadcrumbs in a bowl. Form balls from the mixture, then toss them in the breadcrumbs. Ensure every part of each ball is covered with the breadcrumbs.
2. Preheat your Air Fryer to 200°C/400°F.
3. Place the balls in the basket and cook for 10 minutes.

AIR-FRIED VEGGIE ROLLS

Ready-made rolls never taste as good as homemade. These rolls include veggies and sauce for a tasty kick.

Serving size: 2 portions

TOTAL CALORIES: 640
Fat: 22g | Carbs: 58g | Protein: 55g

INGREDIENTS

- 4 crepes
- ½ zucchini
- 3-4 mushrooms
- 1 carrot
- A pinch of salt
- 2 tbsp. Guacamole

INSTRUCTIONS

1. Grate the zucchini and carrot, and thinly slice the mushrooms. Combine them with the guacamole and salt. Fill a crepe with the mixture. Roll it and repeat the process with the rest of the crepes.
2. Preheat your Air Fryer to 170°C/340°F.
3. Place the rolls in the basket and cook for 10 minutes.

PROTEIN VEGGIE BALLS

An excellent healthy – but still crispy – alternative to deep-fried fries.

Serving size: 3 portions

TOTAL CALORIES: 222
Fat: 8g | Carbs: 29g | Protein: 9g

INGREDIENTS

- 2 cups of cabbage
- ½ cup of oat flour (blended oats)
- ½ cup grated vegan cheese
- 1 tbsp. olive oil
- ½ tsp. salt
- ½ grated eggplant
- 2 tbsp. vegan sour cream

INSTRUCTIONS

1. Preheat your Air Fryer to 200°C/400°F.
2. Combine all ingredients in a bowl. Form irregular balls.
3. Place baking paper in the Air Fryer basket and add the balls.
4. Cook for 10 minutes, then turn them and cook for a further 2 minutes.

EASY FALAFEL TORTILLAS

Fact: you can never have enough falafel balls, and when combined with sauce and tortillas, you'll find the source of true happiness.

Serving size: 4 portions

TOTAL CALORIES: 372
Fat: 7g | Carbs: 52g | Protein: 26g

INGREDIENTS

- 2 cups canned chickpeas
- 1 garlic clove
- ½ onion
- ½ tsp. black pepper
- ½ tsp. salt
- ½ tsp. coriander
- 2 tbsp. sesame seeds
- 4 tortillas
- 4 tsp. Caesar sauce
- 2 tomatoes

INSTRUCTIONS

1. Blend the chickpeas, onion, garlic spices, salt, and sesame seeds together. Blend until smooth. Form 12 small balls from the mixture.
2. Preheat your Air Fryer to 200°C/400°F.
3. Add the balls to the basket and cook for 10 minutes, shaking once.
4. Spread Caesar sauce across every tortilla, then add three falafel balls and tomato slices. Fold the tortillas and serve.

THE AIR FRYER COOKBOOK FOR BEGINNERS

MILLET CAKE FRIES

These salty cakes are easy to prepare and require only four ingredients!

Serving size: 3 portions

TOTAL CALORIES: 376
Fat: 7g | Carbs: 65g | Protein: 14g

INGREDIENTS

- 2 cups millet
- 2 ½ cups veggie broth
- A little salt
- A little curry powder

INSTRUCTIONS

1. Preheat your Air Fryer to 120°C/240°F.
2. Combine the millet and broth in a cooking pan, then add salt and cook in the Air Fryer for 12 minutes.
3. Remove the millet and spread it across a large pan in a 2cm layer.
4. Place the pan in the fridge overnight.
5. In the morning, cut square pieces from the refrigerated mixture and place them in the Air Fryer. Cook for 10 minutes at 200°C/400°F.

VEGAN CHEESE BALLS

These melt-in-your-mouth cheese balls have a crispy outer and gorgeous inner texture. Serve them with a salad or risotto.

Serving size: 3 portions

TOTAL CALORIES: 141
Fat: 5g | Carbs: 19g | Protein: 7g

INGREDIENTS

- A handful of spinach
- 1 carrot
- 100g/3.5oz grated vegan cheese
- 1 boiled potato
- ¼ tsp. salt
- ½ tsp. paprika
- A little oil for the cooking basket

INSTRUCTIONS

1. Grate the carrot and boiled potato. Combine them in a bowl with the vegan cheese, chopped spinach, salt and spices. Form small balls from the mixture with your hands.
2. Preheat your Air Fryer to 180°C/360°F.
3. Add a little oil to the basket, then add the balls and cook for 12 minutes, shaking once.

DEEP-FRIED TEMPEH SALAD

Tempeh is a highly nutritious food with a plant-based origin. It goes particularly well with salad, for a tasty lunch.

Serving size: 2 portions

TOTAL CALORIES: 386
Fat: 27g | Carbs: 15g | Protein: 19g

INGREDIENTS

- 200g/7oz tempeh
- 1 tsp. curcuma
- ¼ tsp. salt
- ¼ tsp. garlic powder
- 2 tsp. water
- 1 lettuce
- 1 tomato
- 2 tbsp. raw pumpkin seeds
- 2 tbsp. olive oil
- A pinch of salt

INSTRUCTIONS

1. Preheat your Air Fryer to 200°C/400°F.
2. Combine the curcuma, garlic, salt and water. Cut the tempeh into 1cm cubes, then cover with the spice mix.
3. Add a little oil to the basket, then place the tempeh pieces in the basket and cook for 10 minutes.
4. Chop the lettuce and tomato. Combine with the pumpkin seeds, dress with olive oil and add the tempeh on top. Sprinkle with salt, if desired.

BLACK BEAN BURGERS

There's no better option for a no-meat burger!

Serving size: 3 portions

TOTAL CALORIES: 438
Fat: 13g | Carbs: 63g | Protein: 19g

INGREDIENTS

- 1 cup canned black beans
- 1 cup canned chickpeas
- ½ cup oat flour (blended oat flakes)
- 2 tbsp. tomato paste
- 1 tbsp. mustard
- 1 tbsp. olive oil
- 1 tsp. paprika
- ½ tsp. salt
- ½ tsp. curry
- 2 burger buns
- 2 tbsp. sriracha
- 1 tomato
- 2 slices beetroot

INSTRUCTIONS

1. Blend the black beans, chickpeas, oat flour, tomato paste, mustard, oil, spices and salt together until well combined.
2. Place baking paper in the Air Fryer basket and then using a spoon add three burger patties.
3. Preheat your Air Fryer to 200°C/400°F.
4. Cook the burger patties for 14 minutes, turning once.
5. Slice the burger bun in half and spread a little sriracha on it. Add the vegan patties, tomato and beetroot slices.

CAULIFLOWER & MUSHROOM RISOTTO

Not every risotto needs to be high in carbs – and this version is low on calories, while still tasty and fulfilling.

Serving size: 3 portions

TOTAL CALORIES: 114
Fat: 5g | Carbs: 12g | Protein: 4g

INGREDIENTS

- 300g/10.5oz cauliflower
- 1 cup veggie broth
- 1 tbsp. avocado oil
- 1 cup wild mushrooms
- 1 clove minced garlic
- 1 onion
- A pinch of salt
- A pinch of black pepper

INSTRUCTIONS

1. Preheat your Air Fryer to 200°C/400°F.
2. Thinly slice the onion and mushrooms.
3. Add a little oil to the basket, then place the onion, garlic and mushrooms in the basket.
4. Cook for 5 minutes.
5. Place the cauliflower in a blender and blend until it achieves a rice-like texture.
6. Take a cooking pan and add the cauliflower rice, veggie broth, onion, garlic, mushrooms, avocado oil, salt and pepper. Mix well, then cook for 8 minutes

MEXICAN CHICKPEA STEW

There's nothing better than a big bowl of hot stew full of hearty veggies.

Serving size: 3 portions

TOTAL CALORIES: 241
Fat: 3g | Carbs: 46g | Protein: 11g

INGREDIENTS

- 1 cup chickpeas
- 3 tbsp. rice
- ½ cup tomato paste
- 2 tbsp. tamari sauce
- 3 cups veggie broth
- 1 carrot
- 1 potato
- ½ onion
- 2 garlic cloves, minced
- 1 chilli pepper
- ½ tsp. salt
- ½ tsp. black pepper

INSTRUCTIONS

1. Dice the carrot and potato. Thinly slice the onion and chilli pepper and mince the garlic.
2. Combine all the ingredients in a cooking pan.
3. Preheat your Air Fryer to 120°C/240°F.
4. Place the cooking pan in the basket and cook for 20 minutes, opening three times to stir the stew.

STUFFED VEGGIE AND NUTS PASTA SHELLS

Shell-shaped pasta lends itself to a variety of dishes – enjoy this inspired vegan combination!

Serving size: 2 portions

TOTAL CALORIES: 634
Fat: 35g | Carbs: 59g | Protein: 22g

INGREDIENTS

- 150g/5.3oz pasta shells
- A handful of spinach
- 150g/5.3oz grated vegan mozzarella
- 1 tbsp. water
- 1 cup basil and tomato sauce
- ½ cup cashews

INSTRUCTIONS

1. Line the pasta shells up in a cooking pan, with the openings face-up.
2. Blend the spinach, mozzarella, cashews and water until well combined, but not smooth. Fill the shells with the spinach mixture. Pour the basil-tomato sauce between the shells.
3. Preheat your Air Fryer to 160°C/320°F.
4. Place the cooking pan in the basket and cook for 12 minutes.

CREAMY VEGAN PIZZA

Pizza ingredients have no boundaries – so alter this recipe to your own taste if necessary.

Serving size: 1 pizza

TOTAL CALORIES: 412
Fat: 11g | Carbs: 17g | Protein: 61g

INGREDIENTS

- 1 pizza base, sized for the basket of your Air Fryer
- 3 tbsp. tomato paste
- 100g/3.5oz grated vegan cheddar cheese
- 5 basil leaves
- ½ tsp. oregano
- 1 bell pepper
- 3 mushrooms

INSTRUCTIONS

1. Preheat your Air Fryer to 200°C/400°F.
2. Spread tomato sauce over the pizza base, then add the cheddar cheese. Thinly slice the bell peppers and mushrooms, then add them to the pizza. Add the basil leaves and sprinkle with oregano.
3. Place the pizza in the basket and cook for 7 minutes.

VEGAN KEBAB TACOS

Crispy corn tacos filled with Turkish-style vegan kebabs.

Serving size: 3 portions

TOTAL CALORIES: 351
Fat: 7g | Carbs: 51g | Protein: 22g

INGREDIENTS

- 5 corn tacos
- 200g/7oz ready-to-bake Turkish-style vegan kebabs
- ½ cup canned corn
- 2 tomatoes
- 1 onion
- 6 pickles
- A little oil for the cooking basket

INSTRUCTIONS

1. Preheat your Air Fryer to 160°C/320°F.
2. Add a little oil to the basket, then place the ready-to-bake kebabs inside and cook for 10 minutes.
3. Dice the tomatoes and onion and thinly slice the pickles. Add the kebab meat to the taco, then tomato, onions and pickles. Sprinkle a little corn on top.

HUMMUS POTATOES

A traditional Spanish-inspired recipe featuring baked potatoes and hummus. Incredibly tasty with an added tomato sauce.

Serving size: 3 portions

TOTAL CALORIES: 192
Fat: 6g | Carbs: 35g | Protein: 5g

INGREDIENTS

- 150g/5.2oz hummus
- 300g/10.5oz potatoes
- A little salt
- A little oil for the cooking basket
- ¼ cup tomato paste

INSTRUCTIONS

1. Preheat your Air Fryer to 200°C/400°F.
2. Cut the potatoes into small cubes and toss with salt.
3. Add a little oil to the basket, then add the potatoes and cook for 15 minutes, shaking the basket once or twice throughout.
4. Spoon hummus into a bowl, then add all the potatoes. Pour the tomato paste over the top.

VEGGIE MEATBALL PASTA

If you're a pasta lover, then vegan meatball pasta should definitely be your next lunch choice.

Serving size: 3 portions

TOTAL CALORIES: 359
Fat: 21g | Carbs: 27g | Protein: 11g

INGREDIENTS

- 3 cups boiled pasta
- 1 cup tomato sauce
- 1 zucchini
- ½ cup sunflower seeds
- 3 tbsp. flour
- ½ tsp. curcuma
- ½ tsp. salt
- 50g/1.7oz canned beetroot

INSTRUCTIONS

1. Preheat your Air Fryer to 200°C/400°F.
2. Blend the zucchini, beetroot, sunflower seeds, flour, curcuma, and salt until smooth.
3. Place baking paper in the Air Fryer basket and form small balls from the mixture.
4. Cook the balls for 10 minutes.
5. Take a cooking pan, add the boiled pasta, tomato sauce and the veggie balls. Place the cooking pan in the basket and cook for a further 5 minutes.

CAULIFLOWER LENTILS STEW

This stew is loaded with healthy and tasty veggies. Lentil recipes are many, but this one stands above the rest for its ease of preparation.

Serving size: 3 portions

TOTAL CALORIES: 212
Fat: 2g | Carbs: 35g | Protein: 15g

INGREDIENTS

- 300g/10.5oz cauliflower
- 1 cup red lentils
- ½ onion
- 1 tsp. curry powder
- ½ tsp. garlic powder
- 2 cups veggie broth
- ½ tsp. salt

INSTRUCTIONS

1. Preheat your Air Fryer to 130°C/260°F.
2. Dice the onion and cauliflower.
3. Take a cooking pan that fits the Air Fryer and combine all the ingredients.
4. Place the cooking pan in the basket and cook for 20 minutes, checking twice to stir.

⑲ ALMOND MEAT SALAD

Almonds are a great source of protein, carbs and healthy fats. This recipe prepares them as a ground meat alternative in a few unique and easy steps.

Serving size: 2 portions

TOTAL CALORIES: 490
Fat: 42g | Carbs: 15g | Protein: 13g

INGREDIENTS

- 100g/3.5oz raw almonds
- 2 tbsp. water
- ½ tsp. Salt
- ½ tsp. paprika
- 2 tbsp. Canned peas
- A handful of rocket
- 1 cucumber
- 1 carrot
- 2 tbsp. Olive oil
- 1 tbsp. Balsamic vinegar
- A pinch of salt

INSTRUCTIONS

1. Preheat your Air Fryer to 200°C/400°F.
2. Blend the almonds, paprika, peas, water and salt until well combined. Take four silicon muffin moulds and fill them with the blended mixture.
3. Add the moulds to the basket and cook for 10 minutes.
4. Prepare the salad: slice the carrot, dice the cucumber and combine with the rocket in a bowl. Dress the salad with balsamic-olive oil dressing, then add the almond meat. Sprinkle with salt and enjoy.

SOY BOLOGNESE PASTA ⑳

This authentic-tasting Bolognese sauce is a must-try for its rich flavours and smooth texture.

Serving size: 3 portions

TOTAL CALORIES: 344
Fat: 4g | Carbs: 57g | Protein: 20g

INGREDIENTS

- 200g/7oz soy crumbs
- 1 cup tomato sauce
- 1 cup veggie broth
- ½ tsp. garlic powder
- 1 onion
- ½ tsp. salt
- 3 cups cooked spaghetti

INSTRUCTIONS

1. Preheat your Air Fryer to 200°C/400°F.
2. Dice the onion. Take a cooking pan and combine the soy crumbs, tomato sauce, veggie broth, garlic powder, salt and onion.
3. Place cook in the Air Fryer for 12 minutes, opening once to stir.
4. Open the basket and add the spaghetti. Stir well and cook for a further 3 minutes.

MUSHROOM PIE

A creamy pie featuring dried mushrooms and a vegan sauce.

Serving size: 4 portions

TOTAL CALORIES: 664
Fat: 35g | Carbs: 67g | Protein: 19g

INGREDIENTS

- 150g/5.3oz dried mushrooms
- 1 cup vegan heavy cream
- ½ cup vegan cheese grated
- A pinch of salt
- A pinch of pepper
- 2 sheets puff pastry

INSTRUCTIONS

1. Combine the mushrooms with the heavy cream, cheese, pepper and salt.
2. Take a cooking pan and place one sheet puff pastry in it. The pastry should cover every side and the base. Fill the pastry with the mushroom mixture and seal with the second sheet of pastry on top. Trim away any excess pastry.
3. Preheat your Air Fryer to 200°C/400°F.
4. Place the cooking pan in the Air Fryer basket and cook for 12 minutes. Take the pie out, let it cool a little, then serve.

SPICY TIKKA MASALA

A vegan version of tikka masala featuring tofu cheese and fragrant spices.

Serving size: 3 portions

TOTAL CALORIES: 192
Fat: 7g | Carbs: 21g | Protein: 12g

INGREDIENTS

- 1 cup rice
- 2 cups veggie broth
- 1 onion
- 1 tsp. Grated ginger
- 1 tsp. Curry
- 1 tsp. Chilli pepper spice
- 1 tsp. Curcuma
- ½ tsp. Salt
- ½ cup vegan cooking cream
- 100g/3.5oz tofu

INSTRUCTIONS

1. Cut the tofu cheese into small cubes.
2. Combine the rice and broth in a cooking pan.
3. Preheat the Air Fryer to 140°C/240°F.
4. Add the cooking pan to the basket and cook for 12 minutes.
5. Combine the spices, salt, heavy cream, and tofu in a saucepan and let simmer.
6. Open the basket and add the tofu and sauce to the rice. Close the basket and cook for a further 5 minutes.

THE AIR FRYER COOKBOOK FOR BEGINNERS

12 | FISH & SEAFOOD

1. Italian shrimp skewers
2. Crunchy hake slices
3. Crispy salmon with veggies
4. White pollock burgers
5. Creamy Argentinian tacos
6. Salmon balls and salad
7. Fried shrimp
8. Crispy stuffed calamari
9. Tuna and cherry tomato pasta
10. Tilapia tomato sticks with risotto
11. Crunchy cod sandwich
12. Salmon taquitos with guacamole
13. Classic fish and chips
14. Tilapia fish
15. Garlic octopus
16. Clam pasta with sauce
17. Cod and tarragon salad
18. Mediterranean branzino and olives
19. Chilli-grilled salmon
20. Rice stew with mini shrimp
21. Crispy fish
22. Mini tuna steaks with pumpkin puree

DON'T FORGET TO GET THE

TOP RECIPES FROM THIS BOOK AS

A DOWNLOADABLE PDF IN COLOUR

FOR FREE!

SCAN THE QR CODE BELOW

SCAN ME

ITALIAN SHRIMP SKEWERS

This recipe features a shrimp and chilli sauce combination that will immediately win you (and your guests!) over.

Serving size: 3 portions

TOTAL CALORIES: 145

Fat: 2g | Carbs: 10g | Protein: 22g

INGREDIENTS

- 300g/10.5oz small shrimp
- ¼ cup sweet chilli sauce
- A pinch of salt
- 6 skewers
- A little oil for the cooking basket

INSTRUCTIONS

1. Preheat your Air Fryer to 200°C/400°F.
2. Place the shrimp on the skewers and spread chilli sauce over them, then sprinkle with salt.
3. Add a little oil to the basket, then add the skewers and cook for 8 minutes.

CRUNCHY HAKE SLICES

Hake fish has a soft texture and only a mild fishy smell, so it's great for home recipes.

Serving size: 3 portions

TOTAL CALORIES: 155

Fat: 2g | Carbs: 18g | Protein: 16g

INGREDIENTS

- 2 pcs. Hake fish
- ½ cup flour
- ½ tsp. Salt
- ½ tsp. Black pepper

INSTRUCTIONS

1. Preheat your Air Fryer to 180°C/360°F.
2. Slice the hake fish into 2cm slices. Discard the head and tail. Toss the fish slices in the flour, ensuring all sides are covered.
3. Place all fish slices in the basket and cook for 12 minutes.

CRISPY SALMON WITH VEGGIES

Salmon is popular due it its high omega-3 content, and this healthy recipe is no exception.

Serving size: 2 portions

TOTAL CALORIES: 301
Fat: 7g | Carbs: 35g | Protein: 25g

INGREDIENTS

- 2 filets of salmon fish
- 1 cup baby potatoes
- 1 cup broccoli
- ½ cup corn flakes
- ½ tsp. Salt
- A little oil for the cooking basket

INSTRUCTIONS

1. Preheat your Air Fryer to 150°C/300°F.
2. Blend the corn flakes and place them in a bowl. Toss the salmon filets in the bowl, ensuring every side of them is covered in corn flakes.
3. Add a little oil to the basket, then place the salmon and veggies inside. Sprinkle with salt.
4. Cook for 15 minutes, checking once to turn the salmon.

WHITE POLLOCK BURGERS

Adding seasoning to your fish is the secret to these delicious burgers.

Serving size: 3 portions

TOTAL CALORIES: 182
Fat: 8g | Carbs: 11g | Protein: 17g

INGREDIENTS

- 2 filets of boneless pollock fish
- 1 tbsp. Butter
- 1 cup breadcrumbs
- 1 egg
- ½ tsp. Salt
- A pinch of pepper
- A pinch of dried mint
- ½ tsp. Onion powder.

INSTRUCTIONS

1. Preheat your Air Fryer to 200°C/400°F.
2. Add baking paper to the basket, then add the pollock filets and cook for 5 minutes.
3. Then, shred the filets into small pieces. Combine with one egg, the breadcrumbs, butter, salt, pepper, onion powder and dried mint in a bowl. Mix well.
4. Form a burger patty from the fish mixture – you should get a total of three burger patties.
5. Add a little oil to the basket, then add the burger patties and cook for 10 minutes. Serve and enjoy.

⑤ CREAMY ARGENTINIAN TACOS

Even non-shrimp lovers will enjoy this creamy mixture of veggies, fresh shrimp and cheese.

Serving size: 3 portions

TOTAL CALORIES: 241
Fat: 4g | Carbs: 23g | Protein: 30g

INGREDIENTS

- 200g/7oz small shrimp
- 1 green pepper
- 1 onion
- 2 cloves of garlic
- 1 tomato
- ½ tsp. Salt
- ½ cup grated cheddar
- 3 tortillas

INSTRUCTIONS

1. Cut the shrimp into very small pieces, so that they look like ground meat. Dice the tomatoes, pepper, onion and garlic.
2. Preheat your Air Fryer to 160°C/320°F.
3. Take a cooking pan and combine the chopped ingredients. Place the cooking pan in the Air Fryer basket and cook for 15 minutes.
4. Take one tortilla and add the cooked shrimp mixture, then add grated cheese and fold it in half. Repeat the process with the remaining two tortillas.
5. Place the tortillas in the basket and cook for 7 minutes.

⑥ SALMON BALLS AND SALAD

Salmon balls are known by various names, including croquets and patties. Traditionally they required a deep-frier, but the Air Fryer bypasses that step.

Serving size: 3 portions

TOTAL CALORIES: 183
Fat: 7g | Carbs: 8g | Protein: 22g

INGREDIENTS

- 300g/10.5oz salmon filets
- ½ onion
- 1 carrot grated
- 2 tbsp. Oat flour
- ½ tsp. Parsley
- ½ tsp. Salt
- ½ tsp. Black pepper
- A handful of lettuce
- 3 tomatoes
- Little olive oil

INSTRUCTIONS

1. Blend the salmon filets with the carrot, oat flour, spices, salt, and onion, until well combined.
2. Preheat your Air Fryer to 200°C/400°F.
3. Form small balls from the salmon mixture – you can use a little extra oat flour if the mixture is sticky.
4. Add a little oil to the basket, then add the balls and cook for 10 minutes, shaking the basket once.
5. Serve with a side dish of lettuce and tomato salad dressed with olive oil.

THE AIR FRYER COOKBOOK FOR BEGINNERS

FRIED SHRIMP

An excellent way to ensure your shrimp are served crispy: crumbed and air-fried.

Serving size: 3 portions

TOTAL CALORIES: 224
Fat: 2g | Carbs: 32g | Protein: 20g

INGREDIENTS

- 200g/7oz small pink shrimp
- 1 tsp. paprika
- 1 cup flour
- 1 egg
- 1 cup breadcrumbs
- ½ tsp. salt

INSTRUCTIONS

1. Combine the flour, paprika and salt in a bowl. In another bowl, beat one egg, and in a third bowl place the bread-crumbs.
2. Take one shrimp and toss it in the flour, then in the egg mixture followed by the breadcrumbs. Repeat for all the shrimp.
3. Preheat your Air Fryer to 200°C/400°F.
4. Add a little oil to the basket, then add the shrimp and cook for 10 minutes, flipping the shrimp halfway through.

CRISPY STUFFED CALAMARI

Fresh calamari should always be bought locally – let the professionals clean and pre-pare it for you.

Serving size: 4 portions

TOTAL CALORIES: 183
Fat: 4g | Carbs: 18g | Protein: 18g

INGREDIENTS

- 4 pcs. calamari (12-15cm long)
- 1 zucchini
- 1 scallion
- 1 tomato
- ½ cup grated parmesan
- 1 cup cooked millet
- ½ tsp. parsley
- ½ tsp. salt
- A little oil for the cooking basket

INSTRUCTIONS

1. Grate the zucchini and tomato. Com-bine them with the parmesan, millet, parsley, chopped scallion and salt. Mix well.
2. Take one piece of calamari and dip it in the zucchini mixture. Repeat the pro-cess with all calamari pieces.
3. Preheat your Air Fryer to 170°C/340°F.
4. Add a little oil to the basket, then add the calamari and cook for 12 minutes, opening once to turn the calamari.

9 TUNA AND CHERRY TOMATO PASTA

(IN MINUTES)
PREP
5
COOK
17

Tuna and pasta are a Mediterranean-inspired match made in heaven.

Serving size: 3 portions

TOTAL CALORIES: 406
Fat: 17g | Carbs: 47g | Protein: 17g

INGREDIENTS

- 200g/7oz tuna
- 1 cup tomato paste
- 1 cup cherry tomatoes
- A couple of basil leaves
- A pinch of salt
- 3 cups cooked pasta
- 3 tbsp. olive oil

INSTRUCTIONS

1. Preheat your Air Fryer to 200°C/400°F.
2. Add a little oil to the basket, then place the tuna and little salt in the basket and cook for 7 minutes.
3. In a cooking pan, combine the pasta with the tomato paste, basil leaves, cherry tomatoes, coked tuna and olive oil. Mix well.
4. Place the cooking pan in the basket and cook for 10 minutes at 130°C/260°F.

10 TILAPIA TOMATO STICKS WITH RISOTTO

(IN MINUTES)
PREP
10
COOK
20

Serve these fish sticks with a veggie risotto and you've got the perfect summer dinner!

Serving size: 3 portions

TOTAL CALORIES: 294
Fat: 8g | Carbs: 32g | Protein: 23g

INGREDIENTS

- 200g/7oz boneless tilapia filets
- ½ cup tomato sauce
- 1 cup breadcrumbs
- A pinch of salt
- 1 cup rice
- 1 cup green beans
- 1 tbsp. butter
- 2 cups veggie broth
- ½ tsp. salt

INSTRUCTIONS

1. Cut the tilapia filets into short 'sticks'. Coat every stick in the tomato sauce and then the breadcrumbs.
2. Preheat your Air Fryer to 200°C/400°F.
3. Add baking paper to the basket then add the tilapia sticks, sprinkling little salt over them. Cook for 8 minutes.
4. In a cooking pan, combine the rice, broth, salt, beans and butter. Place the cooking pan in the basket and cook for 12 minutes at 140°C/280°F. Serve the tilapia tomato sticks with the risotto and enjoy.

THE AIR FRYER COOKBOOK FOR BEGINNERS

CRUNCHY COD SANDWICH

(IN MINUTES)
PREP 10
COOK 5

Every sandwich deserves to be special – and cod and veggies are definitely a unique (and tasty!) sandwich filling.

Serving size: 2 portions

TOTAL CALORIES: 432
Fat: 11g | Carbs: 56g | Protein: 27g

INGREDIENTS

- 4 slices bread
- 2 cod filets
- ½ cup corn flakes
- A pinch of salt
- 2 tbsp. hummus
- 2 fresh mushrooms
- 2 tbsp. olive paste
- A handful of baby spinach

INSTRUCTIONS

1. Sprinkle a little salt over the cod filets, then coat with corn flakes on each side.
2. Preheat your Air Fryer to 180°C/360°F.
3. Place the filets in the basket and cook for 5 minutes on each side.
4. Prepare the sandwiches: spread hummus over one slice of bread then spread olive paste over the other slice of bread. Use the cod filet, mushroom slice and baby spinach as the sandwich filling.

SALMON TAQUITOS WITH GUACAMOLE

(IN MINUTES)
PREP 10
COOK 12

Fresh and tasty taquitos that you can prepare in under 10 minutes.

Serving size: 3 portions

TOTAL CALORIES: 508
Fat: 26g | Carbs: 49g | Protein: 18g

INGREDIENTS

- 150g/5.3oz salmon filet
- 9 mini tortillas
- ½ cup guacamole
- 2 chilli peppers
- A pinch of salt

INSTRUCTIONS

1. Preheat your Air Fryer to 200°C/400°F.
2. Add a little oil to the basket, then place the salmon filets inside and cook for 5 minutes.
3. Shred the filets in a bowl, then add a little salt.
4. Dice the chilli peppers into very small pieces.
5. Take one mini tortilla and spread guacamole over it, then add a little salmon and chilli pepper. Fold the tortilla. Repeat the process with all tortillas.
6. Place the taquitos in the Air Fryer basket and cook for 7 minutes.

CLASSIC FISH AND CHIPS

Feel like you're breaking food-preparation records with this 5-minute fish and chips dish!

Serving size: 2 portions

TOTAL CALORIES: 634
Fat: 35g | Carbs: 59g | Protein: 22g

INGREDIENTS

- 2 white cod fish filets
- 200g/7oz frozen potatoes
- ½ tsp. salt
- 1 egg
- ½ cup flour
- ½ cup breadcrumbs
- 3 tbsp. tzatziki sauce
- A little oil for the cooking basket

INSTRUCTIONS

1. Combine the flour and salt in a bowl. In another bowl, beat the egg, and to a third bowl add the breadcrumbs.
2. Coat one cod filet in the flour, then the egg and finally the breadcrumbs. Repeat the process for the second filet.
3. Preheat your Air Fryer to 200°C/400°F.
4. Add a little oil to the basket, then add the filets and potatoes and cook for 10 minutes. Serve with tzatziki sauce and enjoy.

TILAPIA FISH

Tilapia is a white sea fish that is best served pan fried with salad.

Serving size: 3 portions

TOTAL CALORIES: 176
Fat: 3g | Carbs: 14g | Protein: 23g

INGREDIENTS

- 3 tilapia filets
- ½ tsp. ground cumin
- ¼ tsp. salt
- ½ cup cornflour
- ¼ tsp. black pepper
- Black bean spread

INSTRUCTIONS

1. Preheat your Air Fryer to 200°C/400°F.
2. Combine the spices, salt and cornflour in a bowl. Coat every side of the tilapia fish in the mixture.
3. Place the filets in the Air Fryer basket and cook for 12 minutes, flipping once.
4. Serve with the black bean spread.

GARLIC OCTOPUS

Octopus is great for a dinner with family and friends – serve it with a white wine and lemon water.

Serving size: 2 portions

TOTAL CALORIES: 172

Fat: 8g | Carbs: 1g | Protein: 25g

INGREDIENTS

- 4 octopus legs
- 4 garlic cloves, minced
- A handful of fresh parsley
- 1 tbsp. butter
- A pinch of salt

INSTRUCTIONS

1. Cut the octopus legs into thick slices and chop the parsley. Take a cooking pan and combine the octopus, parsley, garlic, salt and butter.
2. Preheat your Air Fryer to 140°C/280°F.
3. Place the cooking pan in the basket and cook for 12 minutes. Serve with mashed potatoes or carrot puree.

CLAM PASTA WITH SAUCE

Enjoy fresh clams, garlic and semi-cooked pasta in this fun dish.

Serving size: 3 portions

TOTAL CALORIES: 401

Fat: 15g | Carbs: 41g | Protein: 27g

INGREDIENTS

- 500g/17.6oz clamshells
- 3 cups cooked pasta
- 3tbsp. melted butter
- 3 cloves garlic, minced
- ¼ tsp. salt

INSTRUCTIONS

1. Preheat your Air Fryer to 200°C/400°F.
2. Place the clamshells in the basket and cook for 5 minutes.
3. Take a cooking pan and combine the pasta with the butter, garlic and cooked clams.
4. Add the pan to the basket and cook for a further 5 minutes.

COD AND TARRAGON SALAD

For a fresh, healthy meal, look no further than cod served with salad and tarragon sauce.

Serving size: 2 portions

TOTAL CALORIES: 265
Fat: 13g | Carbs: 11g | Protein: 24g

INGREDIENTS

- 2 cod filets
- ¼ cup heavy cream
- ¼ cup veggie broth
- 3 sticks tarragon
- 1 clove minced garlic
- 1 tsp. corn starch
- ¼ tsp. salt
- A pinch of pepper
- 1 small Chinese lettuce
- 1 green pepper
- 1 tbsp. olive oil

INSTRUCTIONS

1. Preheat your Air Fryer to 120°C/240°F.
2. Add a little oil to the basket, then place the cod filets in the basket with little salt. Cook for 10 minutes.
3. In the meantime, combine the heavy cream, veggie broth, salt, garlic, pepper, corn starch, and tarragon pieces in a saucepan. Bring the mixture to a boil, stirring it constantly.
4. Slice the lettuce and pepper, then place in a bowl. Add the cooked cod filets and dress the salad them with tarragon sauce and olive oil.

MEDITERRANEAN BRANZINO AND OLIVES

Branzino fish is best when fresh – always check your local market first!

Serving size: 2 portions

TOTAL CALORIES: 370
Fat: 21g | Carbs: 5g | Protein: 37g

INGREDIENTS

- 2 branzino fish
- 100g/3.5oz green olives
- 2 garlic cloves
- Salt, to taste
- 2 tbsp. olive oil
- Rosemary sticks

INSTRUCTIONS

1. Brush olive oil over the fish then sprinkle with salt. To the middle of the fish add one garlic clove and one rosemary stick.
2. Preheat your Air Fryer to 170°C/340°F.
3. Place the grill tray in the Air Fryer basket and add the branzino fish. Cook for 12 minutes, turning once. Serve with fresh olives and enjoy.

CHILLI-GRILLED SALMON

If you're a lover of spicy food then this quick recipe is for you!

Serving size: 3 portions

TOTAL CALORIES: 170
Fat: 8g | Carbs: 3g | Protein: 22g

INGREDIENTS

- 3 salmon filets
- 1 tbsp. chilli pepper
- 2 tbsp. BBQ sauce
- ¼ tsp. salt
- 1 tbsp. olive oil

INSTRUCTIONS

1. Preheat your Air Fryer to 200°C/400°F.
2. Place the grill tray in the Air Fryer basket.
3. Combine all ingredients together in a bowl, ensure the salmon is well coated.
4. Place the filets on the grill and cook for 8 minutes.

RICE STEW WITH MINI SHRIMP

This shrimp stew is rich in flavour and easy to prepare. Save it for a treat after a long and busy day.

Serving size: 2 portions

TOTAL CALORIES: 333
Fat: 2g | Carbs: 55g | Protein: 25g

INGREDIENTS

- 200g/7oz extra-small shrimp
- 1 cup rice
- 2 cups gazpacho juice
- 1 minced garlic clove
- ¼ tsp. salt
- 1 green pepper
- 5 brussels sprouts
- 1 tsp. sugar

INSTRUCTIONS

1. Preheat your Air Fryer to 140°C/280°F.
2. Slice the pepper and cut the brussels sprouts in half.
3. Take a cooking pan and combine all ingredients.
4. Place the cooking pan in the basket and cook for 14 minutes, stirring once.

CRISPY FISH

(IN MINUTES)
PREP
10
COOK
12

Mackerel has high levels of omega-3, and this recipe will help you produce a true fish-based masterpiece.

Serving size: 2 portions

TOTAL CALORIES: 265
Fat: 17g | Carbs: 0g | Protein: 25g

INGREDIENTS

- 2 mackerel filets
- 1 tsp. curry powder
- 1 tsp. oregano
- 1 tsp. white pepper
- ½ tsp. salt
- 2 tbsp. olive oil
- 1 lemon

INSTRUCTIONS

1. Preheat your Air Fryer to 180°C/360°F.
2. Cut the mackerel fish into two horizontal pieces. Dress them with the olive oil, spices and salt.
3. Place the grill tray in the Air Fryer basket and add the mackerel pieces, skin side up.
4. Cook for 12 minutes. Serve with lemon slices.

MINI TUNA STEAKS WITH PUMPKIN PUREE

(IN MINUTES)
PREP
5
COOK
15

Tuna is popular for a reason – it has a lower fat percentage than many other types of fish and is incredibly nutritious.

Serving size: 2 portions

TOTAL CALORIES: 296
Fat: 8g | Carbs: 33g | Protein: 24g

INGREDIENTS

- 200gr/7oz tuna steak
- 1 cup pumpkin puree
- 1 boiled potato
- 2 tbsp. heavy cream
- ½ onion
- ¼ tsp. salt
- 2 tbsp. sweet chilli sauce
- A little oil for the cooking basket

INSTRUCTIONS

1. Cut the tuna steak into 2cm thick slices. Place in a bowl and combine with the chilli sauce and a pinch of salt. Mix well.
2. Preheat your Air Fryer to 160°C/320°F.
3. Add a little oil to the basket, then add the tuna steaks and bake for 10 minutes.
4. In the meantime, place the pumpkin puree, potato, onion, heavy cream and salt in a blender. Blend until smooth.
5. Place the pumpkin puree mixture in a saucepan and simmer for 5 minutes.
6. Serve a couple of mini tuna steaks with the pumpkin puree and enjoy.

THE AIR FRYER COOKBOOK FOR BEGINNERS

13 | DESSERTS

1. Turkish stuffed pears
2. Chocolate pudding with berries
3. Raspberry cake
4. Chocolate cake
5. Carrot cake
6. Peanut butter snack balls
7. Coconut and hazelnut cups
8. Strawberry crepes
9. Churros with chocolate cream
10. Chocolate-filled balls
11. Strawberry-filled moons
12. Mini sherbet doughnuts
13. Pumpkin and cashew cups
14. Banana oat muffins
15. Spicy oatmeal cookies
16. Peach pie
17. Red beetroot cake with white icing
18. Almond lakes with jam
19. Keto chocolate brownies
20. High protein Gugelhupf

DON'T FORGET TO GET THE

TOP RECIPES FROM THIS BOOK AS

A DOWNLOADABLE PDF IN COLOUR

FOR FREE!

SCAN THE QR CODE BELOW

SCAN ME

TURKISH STUFFED PEARS

This unorthodox recipe sees pears stuffed with dried fruit and rice – a real sweet treat.

Serving size: 3 portions

TOTAL CALORIES: 470
Fat: 18g | Carbs: 68g | Protein: 7g

INGREDIENTS

- 3 medium sized pears
- 3 tbsp. rice
- 3 tbsp. dried cranberries
- ½ cup crushed walnuts
- ½ cup orange juice
- 3 tbsp. vanilla sugar
- 3 tbsp. honey

INSTRUCTIONS

1. Peel the pear and remove the core. You can use a knife or core remover if you have one.
2. Combine the rice, cranberries, blended walnuts, orange juice and honey.
3. Stuff every pear with the mixture, then place them in the Air Fryer basket and sprinkle with vanilla sugar.
4. Preheat your Air Fryer to 120°C/240°F.
5. Cook the pears for 18 minutes.

CHOCOLATE PUDDING WITH BERRIES

Yes, puddings can be prepared in your Air Fryer!

Serving size: 4 portions

TOTAL CALORIES: 332
Fat: 8g | Carbs: 33g | Protein: 8g

INGREDIENTS

- 2 bananas
- 100g/3.5oz milk chocolate
- 3 tbsp. corn starch
- 2 cups milk
- 4 circular biscuits
- 1 cup raspberries

INSTRUCTIONS

1. Blend the banana, chocolate, cornstarch and milk, until well combined.
2. Take four silicon muffin moulds and place one biscuit at the bottom of each. Add a couple of raspberries. Then, pour the chocolate mixture over the raspberries.
3. Preheat your Air Fryer to 140°C/280°F.
4. Place the silicon moulds in the basket and cook for 12 minutes.

RASPBERRY CAKE

3

A delightful treat featuring wild raspberries and a sugar coating – perfect with a cup of coffee.

Serving size: 6 portions

TOTAL CALORIES: 293
Fat: 20g | Carbs: 21g | Protein: 5.2g

INGREDIENTS

- 3 eggs
- 3 tbsp. sugar
- 1 cup raspberries
- 1 cup flour
- 1 tsp. baking powder
- ½ cup sunflower oil
- ½ cup Greek yogurt

INSTRUCTIONS

1. Whisk the eggs, then add the sugar and continue whisking until the sugar has melted. Add the flour, Greek yogurt, oil, and baking powder. Whisk until the mixture is well combined.
2. Take a cooking pan and place baking paper in it. At the bottom of the pan place the raspberries. Then, cover them with the cake mixture.
3. Preheat your Air Fryer to 170°C/340°F.
4. Place the cooking pan in the basket and cook for 20 minutes.

CHOCOLATE CAKE

4

This decadent chocolate cake is rich and creamy, and perfect for birthday celebrations.

Serving size: 6 portions

TOTAL CALORIES: 524
Fat: 34g | Carbs: 40g | Protein: 11g

INGREDIENTS

- 1 cup flour
- ½ cup sugar
- 2 tsp. baking powder
- 1 tsp. baking soda
- 3 eggs
- 1 cup milk
- ½ cup oil
- 3 tbsp. raw cocoa powder
- 1 tsp. vanilla extract
- 100g/3.5oz chocolate
- 1 cup heavy cream

INSTRUCTIONS

1. Start by whisking the eggs and adding the sugar. Whisk until the sugar is melted. Add the flour, cocoa powder, baking powder, baking soda, milk, oil and vanilla extract. Mix well.
2. Take a cooking pan and place baking paper in it. Add the cake mixture.
3. Preheat your Air Fryer to 170°C/340°F.
4. Add the cooking pan to the basket and cook for 20 minutes.
5. In the meantime, prepare the icing. Bring the heavy cream to the boil in a saucepan, together with the chocolate. When it begins to boil, set it aside and stir very quickly until the mixture is well combined.
6. Take the cake out of the pan and slowly add the icing.

CARROT CAKE

The mascarpone icing is the star of this dessert, although the soft, sweet cake filling is a close second!

Serving size: 6 portions

TOTAL CALORIES: 748
Fat: 48g | Carbs: 61g | Protein: 16g

INGREDIENTS

- 2 large carrots
- 2 eggs
- 1 cup yogurt
- 1 cup flour
- ½ cup blended walnuts
- ½ cup muscovado sugar
- 1 tsp. cinnamon
- ½ cup oil
- ½ tsp. grated nutmeg
- 1 tsp. baking powder
- 1 tsp. vanilla extract
- 200g mascarpone
- 2 tbsp. honey

INSTRUCTIONS

1. Grate the carrots. Whisk the eggs and add sugar, until well combined. Then add the flour, walnuts, yoghurt, carrots, cinnamon, oil, nutmeg, baking powder and vanilla extract. Mix well.
2. Place baking paper in the cooking pan and pour in the carrot mixture.
3. Preheat your Air Fryer to 180°C/360°F.
4. Place the cooking pan in the basket and cook for 22 minutes.
5. In the meantime, whisk the mascarpone and honey together.
6. Take the cake out of the pan, remove the baking paper and let it cool.
7. Ice with the mascarpone.

PEANUT BUTTER SNACK BALLS

Perfect as a snack between meals, or for afternoon tea.

Serving size: 6 portions

TOTAL CALORIES: 242
Fat: 8g | Carbs: 34g | Protein: 9g

INGREDIENTS

- 4 tbsp. peanut butter
- 1 egg
- 2 tbsp. sesame seeds
- 3 tbsp. maple syrup
- 1 cup oat flakes
- 1 tsp. raw cocoa

INSTRUCTIONS

1. Preheat your Air Fryer to 180°C/360°F.
2. Combine all ingredients and form small balls.
3. Place baking paper in the Air Fryer basket and add all the balls. Cook for 15 minutes.

COCONUT AND HAZELNUT CUPS

These cupcakes are perfect for travel, and delicious!

Serving size: 6 portions

TOTAL CALORIES: 556

Fat: 32g | Carbs: 56g | Protein: 8g

INGREDIENTS

- 3 eggs
- ½ cup dark sugar
- 1 cup flour
- 1 cup coconut flakes
- ½ cup milk
- 1 tsp. baking powder
- ½ cup melted coconut oil
- 1 tsp. vanilla extract
- ½ cup blended hazelnuts

INSTRUCTIONS

1. Whisk the eggs until they foam. Add the sugar, continually whisking. Slowly whisk all remaining ingredients into the mixture.
2. Fill 6 silicon muffin moulds with the mixture.
3. Preheat your Air Fryer to 200°C/400°F.
4. Place the moulds in the basket and cook for 18 minutes.

STRAWBERRY CREPES

This quick and easy traditional Greek recipe is perfect for special occasions.

Serving size: 6 portions

TOTAL CALORIES: 334

Fat: 10g | Carbs: 51g | Protein: 8g

INGREDIENTS

- 6 crepes
- 1 cup strawberries
- ½ cup strawberry jam
- ½ cup raw almonds
- ½ cup vanilla sugar

INSTRUCTIONS

1. Preheat your Air Fryer to 200°C/400°F.
2. Spread strawberry jam over every crepe, then add a couple of almonds. Cut the strawberries and add to the crepe. Roll the crepe and repeat for all.
3. Place the crepes in the Air Fryer basket and sprinkle with vanilla sugar. Cook for 7 minutes.

CHURROS WITH CHOCOLATE CREAM

Churros are traditionally prepared via deep-frying, but the Air Fryer replaces this step entirely.

Serving size: 6 portions

TOTAL CALORIES: 325
Fat: 13g | Carbs: 45g | Protein: 4.6g

INGREDIENTS

- 1 cup flour
- 1 cup water
- 70g/2.46oz butter
- 2 tbsp. sugar
- A little salt
- 2 eggs
- 1 tbsp. cinnamon
- ½ cup sugar

INSTRUCTIONS

1. Combine the water, butter, salt, sugar, and salt in a saucepan. Bring the mixture to the boil, then remove from the heat. Mix well with a silicon spatula, then gradually add the flour. Mix for three minutes. When the mixture is no longer sticky, transfer it to a silicon bowl.
2. Whisk the eggs and slowly add them to the silicon bowl, stirring constantly. When all ingredients are combined, transfer them to a piping bag with a star shaped tip.
3. Preheat your Air Fryer to 190°C/380°F.
4. Pipe the churros into the basket (approx. 5cm long). Cook for 15 minutes.
5. In the meantime, combine the sugar and cinnamon, and when the churros are ready toss them in the sugar mixture.
6. Serve with chocolate cream and enjoy.

CHOCOLATE-FILLED BALLS

Crunchy on the outside and meltingly good on the inside – these balls are an easy everyday treat.

Serving size: 6 portions

TOTAL CALORIES: 230
Fat: 7.5g | Carbs: 35g | Protein: 5g

INGREDIENTS

- 100g/3.5oz chocolate cubes
- 1 cup flour
- 2 tbsp. sugar
- ½ cup milk
- 1 egg
- 2 tbsp. olive oil
- 1 tsp. baking powder
- A little powdered sugar

INSTRUCTIONS

1. Combine the flour, milk, oil, sugar and baking powder. Knead the mixture well.
2. Take one chocolate cube and 1 tbsp. of dough. Form a ball of dough around the chocolate cube, positioning it in the middle of the ball. Repeat for all chocolate pieces.
3. Preheat your Air Fryer to 200°C/400°F.
4. Place the balls in silicone ball moulds. Cook for 12 minutes. Serve with powdered sugar and enjoy.

THE AIR FRYER COOKBOOK FOR BEGINNERS

STRAWBERRY-FILLED MOONS

Strawberry and vanilla is the true power couple of flavours, and they are suitably united in this recipe in the form of half-moon pastries.

Serving size: 6 portions

TOTAL CALORIES: 232
Fat: 12g | Carbs: 26g | Protein: 4g

INGREDIENTS

- 1 sheet puff pastry
- ½ cup vanilla cream
- 6 large strawberries

INSTRUCTIONS

1. Cut the puff pastry into 3-inch circles.
2. To each pastry circle place the vanilla cream, then a strawberry. Fold each pastry circle in half and seal the edges with the help of your fingers.
3. Preheat your Air Fryer to 200°C/400°F.
4. Place all pastries in the basket and bake for 12 minutes.

MINI SHERBET DOUGHNUTS

These juicy doughnuts are a powerful energy source and are best served in small numbers as a snack between meals.

Serving size: 10 portions

TOTAL CALORIES: 138
Fat: 2.5g | Carbs: 35g | Protein: 3g

INGREDIENTS

- 1 cup flour
- 1 tbsp. sugar
- A pinch of salt
- 1 tsp. baking powder
- 1 egg
- ½ cup milk
- 1 tbsp. melted butter
- 2 cups water
- 1 cup sugar
- ¼ cup lemon juice

INSTRUCTIONS

1. Combine the flour, sugar, salt, baking powder, egg, milk, and melted butter. Mix well.
2. Fill a silicone doughnut mould with the batter.
3. Preheat your Air Fryer to 180°C/360°F.
4. Place the silicon moulds in the basket and cook for 12 minutes.
5. In the meantime, prepare the sherbet. Combine the sugar, water and lemon juice in a saucepan. Bring the mixture to a simmer, then set aside to cool.
6. When the sherbet has cooled, place the doughnuts in the mixture and let them soak for 2-3 minutes.

⑬ PUMPKIN AND CASHEW CUPS

Orange colouring is perfect for autumn decor, and these cupcakes will do your festive baking proud!

Serving size: 6 portions

TOTAL CALORIES: 520
Fat: 35g | Carbs: 39g | Protein: 12g

INGREDIENTS

- 1 cup pumpkin puree
- ½ cup oil
- 1 cup flour
- 1 tsp. baking powder
- 1 cup crushed cashews
- 2 eggs
- 2 tbsp. sugar
- 1 tsp. cinnamon

INSTRUCTIONS

1. Whisk the eggs, then slowly add the sugar. Continue to whisk until the sugar has melted. Add the pumpkin puree, then the flour, baking powder, oil, cinnamon and cashews. Mix well.
2. Take 6 normal sized silicon cupcake moulds and fill them with the mixture.
3. Preheat your Air Fryer to 200°C/400°F.
4. Place the cupcake moulds in the basket and cook for 15 minutes.

⑭ BANANA OAT MUFFINS

For healthy eaters who love a treat, these muffins are the perfect option.

Serving size: 6 portions

TOTAL CALORIES: 392
Fat: 22g | Carbs: 33g | Protein: 15g

INGREDIENTS

- 2 bananas
- 1 cup oats
- 1 cup peanuts
- 3 eggs
- ½ cup chocolate chips, with stevia

INSTRUCTIONS

1. Grind the peanuts into very small pieces. Combine with the oat flakes, mashed banana, eggs and chocolate chips. Mix well.
2. Take 6 silicone muffin moulds and fill them with the mixture.
3. Preheat your Air Fryer to 160°C/320°F.
4. Place the muffin moulds in the basket and cook for 12 minutes.

SPICY OATMEAL COOKIES

Oatmeal cookies are an excellent on-the-go dessert option, and this recipe requires only a few basic ingredients.

Serving size: 4 portions

TOTAL CALORIES: 608
Fat: 35g | Carbs: 52g | Protein: 20g

INGREDIENTS

- 1 cup oat flakes
- 1 egg
- 4 tbsp. hazelnut butter
- 2 tbsp. date syrup
- 1 cup almond flakes
- ½ tsp. baking powder
- ½ tsp. ginger powder
- ½ tsp. cinnamon
- ½ tsp. ground nutmeg

INSTRUCTIONS

1. Preheat your Air Fryer to 180°C/360°F.
2. Combine all ingredients.
3. Add baking paper to the basket and scoop small amounts of the cookie mix into the basket, making sure they are kept separate from each other.
4. Cook the cookies for 12 minutes.

PEACH PIE

A sweet-and-sour treat featuring peaches, heavy cream and puff pastry.

Serving size: 6 portions

TOTAL CALORIES: 480
Fat: 23.3g | Carbs: 61g | Protein: 7.6g

INGREDIENTS

- 3 peaches
- 4 tbsp. sugar
- 1 tsp. vanilla extract
- ½ cup heavy cream
- 2 puff pastry sheets

INSTRUCTIONS

1. Cut the peaches into half-moon shaped slices. Combine them with the sugar, vanilla and heavy cream. Let the mixture simmer in a saucepan for 5 minutes.
2. Take a cooking pan and line it with one sheet of puff pastry. Add the peach mixture and seal the pie with another sheet of puff pastry over the top. Trim any excess pastry.
3. Preheat your Air Fryer to 200°C/400°F.
4. Place the cooking pan in the basket and cook for 12 minutes.

RED BEETROOT CAKE WITH WHITE ICING

This dessert looks as good as it tastes!

Serving size: 6 portions

TOTAL CALORIES: 377
Fat: 15g | Carbs: 53g | Protein: 7.5g

INGREDIENTS

- 200g/7oz boiled beetroot
- 1 cup flour
- 1tbsp. baking powder
- 3 eggs
- ¼ cup melted butter
- ½ cup brown sugar
- 2 tbsp. hazelnut butter
- ½ tsp. ground nutmeg
- 1 cup ready-made vanilla pudding

INSTRUCTIONS

1. Place the beetroot in a food processor and blend it until it is pureed.
2. Beat the eggs with a hand mixer. Slowly add the sugar, flour, melted butter, beetroot puree, hazelnut butter, nutmeg and baking powder.
3. Take a cooking pan and place baking paper in it. Pour the cake mixture in.
4. Preheat your Air Fryer to 180°C/360°F.
5. Place the cooking pan in the basket and bake for 20 minutes.
6. When the cake is ready, take it out of the pan and let it cool.
7. Cut the cake in half horizontally and spread the bottom part of the cake with vanilla pudding. Replace the top half of the cake, cut generous pieces and serve.

ALMOND LAKES WITH JAM

With a jam-filled 'lake' in the centre of each biscuit, these are sure to be a hit.

Serving size: 6 portions

TOTAL CALORIES: 550
Fat: 35g | Carbs: 45g | Protein: 11g

INGREDIENTS

- 1 cup blended raw almonds
- 1 cup flour
- ½ cup butter
- 1 egg
- 3 tbsp. sugar
- 1 tsp. vanilla extract
- A pinch of salt
- Jam of choice

INSTRUCTIONS

1. Combine the almonds, flour, sugar, butter, egg, vanilla and salt. Knead well.
2. Form small circles from the dough, then press down in the centre of each circle with your finger.
3. Preheat your Air Fryer to 200°C/400°F.
4. Place the dough circles in the basket and cook for 10 minutes. Take them out and add a little jam to the dip in the centre of each circle.

THE AIR FRYER COOKBOOK FOR BEGINNERS

KETO CHOCOLATE BROWNIES

 19

A glorious keto brownie recipe – there's no sugar or flour, but lots of flavour!

Serving size: 6 portions

TOTAL CALORIES: 322
Fat: 28g | Carbs: 9g | Protein: 9g

INGREDIENTS

- 3 eggs
- 3 tbsp. butter
- 2 tbsp. stevia
- 1 cup almond flour
- 1 tsp. baking powder
- 1 tsp. vanilla extract
- 2 tbsp. raw cocoa
- ½ cup blended peanuts

INSTRUCTIONS

1. Beat the eggs and slowly add the stevia, then the almond flour. Beat for a further minute. Add the rest of the ingredients and mix well.
2. Place baking paper in the cooking pan and fill with the brownie mixture.
3. Preheat the Air Fryer to 180°C/360°F.
4. Add the cooking pan to the basket and cook for 20 minutes, checking once. Serve with berries and enjoy.

HIGH PROTEIN GUGELHUPF

 20

A Gugelhupf cake can feature a variety of flavours, and this recipe is sugar free and high in protein.

Serving size: 6 portions

TOTAL CALORIES: 190
Fat: 12g | Carbs: 6g | Protein: 14g

INGREDIENTS

- 2 eggs
- 1 tsp. baking soda
- 2 scoops vanilla whey protein
- ½ cup chia flour
- 1 banana
- ½ cup milk

INSTRUCTIONS

1. Combine all ingredients in a blender.
2. Take a silicone Gugelhupf mould and pour the mixture in.
3. Preheat your Air Fryer to 180°C/360°F.
4. Place the mould in the basket and bake for 15 minutes. Take it out and let it cool. Serve and enjoy.

ABOUT THE AUTHOR

We are Fearne Prentice!

A group of Chefs & Recipe Writers decided to team up
and work together to create the best UK Cookbooks
on the market!

See, by working together we can alleviate each
other's weaknesses and create the most delicious
recipes for you to enjoy.

Whether it's needing some UK Air Fryer classics to spice
up your parties, or some slow cooker favorites to warm
your winters we can promise we've got you covered.

We'd also LOVE to hear your feedback and see your
pictures when you create our recipes! Please share
them with us and leave a review!

Now, enough talking, it's time to get back to cooking!

Don't forget to check out these other books by Fearne Prentice!

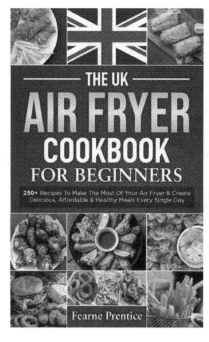  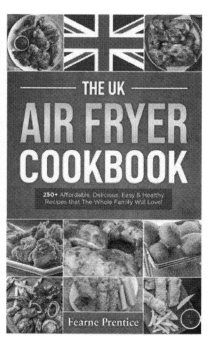

Printed in Great Britain
by Amazon

15335401R00088